D0469816

Cryptocurrency:

Mining, Investing and Trading Bitcoin, Ethereum, Litecoin, Ripple, Dash, Gridcoin, Iota, Digibyte, Dogecoin, Emercoin, Putincoin, Auroracoin and others [2nd edition]

Table of Contents

IMPORTANT NOTE...10

INTRODUCTION..11

CHAPTER 1: THE BASICS OF CRYPTOGRAPHIC
CURRENCY...12

HAVE CRYPTOCURRENCIES LIVED UP TO THE HYPE? 13

STRONGHOLDS.. 16

THE EDGE OVER FIAT CURRENCIES.................................... 17

WHAT MINERS DO.. 18

ACCEPTABILITY 21

THE NECESSITY OF TIMESTAMPING 21

MINOR SETBACKS 22

FINAL THOUGHTS 23

CHAPTER 2: BITCOIN, ETHEREUM AND LITECOIN.................24

HOW BITCOIN IS WIRED.. 24

UNMASKING THE BITCOIN INVENTOR 25

THE POPULATION THAT HAS EMBRACED THE BITCOIN............ 25

BITCOIN'S ECONOMIC POWER 26

INVESTING IN BITCOIN 28

THE MECHANISM OF MINING BITCOINS.......................... 30

CONTROVERSIES 32

ETHEREUM (ETH)... 33

A UNIVERSAL COMPUTER SYSTEM 34

THE ANNALS OF ETHEREUM 35

THE ETHEREUM BLOCKCHAIN 36

MINING OF ETHER.. 36

THE ETHEREUM VIRTUAL MACHINE................................ 36

THE ETHEREUM COMMUNITY 37

THE EXPLOSIVE RELEVANCE OF SMART CONTRACTS 38

THE HACK... 38

THE EMERGENCE OF ETHEREUM CLASSIC 39

TOTAL MARKET VALUE 39

ETHEREUM WALLETS 40

USABILITY OF ETHEREUM 40

DIFFERENCES BETWEEN BITCOIN AND ETHEREUM 41

ETHEREUM'S FUTURE 42

LITECOIN (LTC) 43

REASONS FOR LITECOIN'S INVENTION 44

LITECOIN'S CORE DEVELOPERS 44

WHAT IS THE TOTAL NUMBER OF LITECOINS? 45

THE VALUE OF LITECOIN 46

PURCHASING LITECOINS (WEBSITES AND EXCHANGE PLATFORMS) 46

LITECOIN'S MINING PROCEDURES 46

ADDITIONAL BENEFITS 50

BLOCKCHAIN 50

WALLET ENCRYPTION 51

MAINTENANCE OF A SMALL MINING POOL 51

MINING DIFFICULTY 51

CONCLUSION 51

CHAPTER 3: RIPPLE (XRP)..53

THE ANNALS OF RIPPLE AND ITS GRADUAL DEVELOPMENT ... 54

INTEREST IN THE BANKING SECTOR 55

MECHANISMS 56

THE ARCHITECTURE OF RIPPLE'S PROTOCOL 57

IDEOLOGY 60

ACCEPTABILITY 61

COMPARISONS TO OTHER DIGITAL CURRENCIES. 62

REACTIONS TO XRP 62

CHAPTER 4: THE DASH CRYPTOCURRENCY..........................64

THE ANNALS OF DASH 64

MARKET CAPITALIZATION 65

DASH COIN SUPPLY 66

MINERS AND MASTERNODES 66

FUNDING AND MANAGEMENT 67

THE DASH TECHNOLOGY 69

DASH'S ACQUISITION OPTIONS 70

DASH WALLETS 70

THE FUTURE OF THE DASH CRYPTOCURRENCY 71

FINAL THOUGHTS 78

CHAPTER 5: ZCASH (ZEC)..80

THE ANNALS OF ZCASH 83

CORE COMPONENTS 84

HOW ZK-SNARKS ARE APPLIED TO CREATE A SHIELDED TRANSACTION 86

MINING ZCASH 87

FUTURE APPLICATIONS OF ZK-SNARKS 87

CHAPTER 6: THE GRIDCOIN (GRC)............................89

THE ANNALS OF GRIDCOIN 90

FEATURES 90

EARNING GRIDCOIN AS A REWARD FOR BOINC COMPUTATIONS 91

THE RELEVANCE OF GRIDCOIN 92

CHAPTER 7: THE IOTA CRYPTOCURRENCY...............93

THE IOTA TOKEN 94

THE IOTA TEAM AND FOUNDATION 95

RUNNING AN IOTA WALLET 95

CHAPTER 8: DIGIBYTE (DGB)....................................97

THE ANNALS OF DIGIBYTE 97

FEATURES 98

MINING ALGORITHMS 99

COMMUNITIES 99

WALLETS 100

EXCHANGE PLATFORMS 100

IMPACT 100

CHAPTER 9: DOGECOIN (DOGE)………………..…………**102**

THE ANNALS OF DOGECOIN 102

THE DOGECHAIN.. 103

BLOCKS 103

EXCHANGE PLATFORMS 104

MINING 104

CAMPAIGNS 105

VERDICT... 106

CHAPTER 10: THE BURSTCOIN (BURST)…………………...**107**

THE ANNALS OF BURSTCOIN... 107

THE VALUE OF BURSTCOIN.. 108

THE BURSTCOIN BLOCKCHAIN.. 108

SECURITY 109

MINING 109

MINING POOLS... 109

FEATURES OF BURSTCOIN 110

CROWDFUNDING 110

HOW TRANSACTIONS ARE CONDUCTED IN THE BURSTCOIN
NETWORK 111

THE BURST NATION 111

CHAPTER 11: EMERCOIN (EMC)…………………………….**116**

THE ANNALS OF EMERCOIN 117

WALLETS.. 121

HOW TO ACQUIRE EMERCOINS 122

THE USABILITY OF EMERCOIN.. 122

DECENTRALIZATION OF DOMAIN NAMES 122

INTERESTS 123

CHAPTER 12: PUTINCOIN………………………………….**124**

BENEFITS OF PUTINCOIN 124

SECURITY 124

THE PUTINCOIN TECHNOLOGY 125

DECENTRALIZATION... 125

DEVELOPMENT 125

CHAPTER 13: PEERCOIN (PPC)...126

CREATION/ MINING OF PEERCOINS 127

PROTECTION OF PEERCOIN 127

DISTINGUISHING FEATURES 128

FEATURES 128

REDUCED ENERGY CONSUMPTION 129

THE INFLATION MECHANISM 129

BEYOND ONLINE PLATFORMS 130

MINTING PEERCOIN 131

CHAPTER 14: AURORACOIN (AUR)....................................132

THE ANNALS OF AURORACOIN 132

THE SPREAD OF AURORACOIN 133

FEATURES 134

THE AIRDROP 134

THE AURORACOIN FOUNDATION 135

USES OF AURORACOIN 135

TRANSFER AND RECEPTION OF AURORACOINS AS A PAYMENT OPTION 136

WAYS TO ACQUIRE AURORACOIN 136

THE DEVELOPMENT OF AURORACOIN 136

CHAPTER 15: NXT (NXT)...139

THE ANNALS OF NXT 139

FEATURES 140

VOTING SYSTEM 142

MONETARY PROGRAM 142

PROOF OF STAKE 142

TRANSPARENT FORGING 142

ACCESSIBILITY 142

THE NXT BLOCKCHAIN 142

COMMUNITY 143

CIRCULATION 143

CHAPTER 16: MONERO (XMR)..**144**

THE ANNALS OF MONERO 145

FEATURES 146

THE MONERO MARKET 147

DECENTRALIZATION AND MINING 148

SUCCINCT EXPLANATION OF MONERO'S IMPORTANT ASPECTS
.... 148

VERDICT.. 156

CHAPTER 17: NEM (XEM)..**158**

THE ANNALS OF NEM 158

THE ALPHA AND BETA VERSIONS.. 160

THE STRUCTURE OF NEM 160

FEATURES 160

FOOD FOR THOUGHT 162

CHAPTER 18: DIGITAL NOTE (XDN)....................................**170**

FEATURES 170

WALLETS 171

ACQUIRING XDN 171

EXCHANGE PLATFORMS 172

CHAPTER 19: YBCOIN..**173**

MINING PROCESS 174

FEATURES 174

PROCESS OF DEVELOPMENT 174

**CHAPTER 20: UNDERSTANDING BLOCKCHAIN
TECHNOLOGY**..**176**

BLOCKCHAIN TECHNOLOGY 176

KEY FEATURES 177

ORGANIZATIONS THAT HAVE ALREADY TAPPED INTO THE
RESOURCES OF BOCKCHAIN TECHNOLOGY 185

THE PLAUSIBLE RELEVANCE OF THE BLOCKCHAIN 185

PROBABLE DOWNSIDE 190

GLOSSARY..**194**

REFERENCES..**206**

Author's Note..**229**

IMPORTANT NOTE

Firstly, I want to thank you for purchasing this book.

I hope you enjoy this book learn more about cryptocurrencies.

There is a glossary near the end of the book that you can refer to if any words or technical terms are not clear. I have also included many pages of references at the end of the book that you can look at if you want to read or learn more.

INTRODUCTION

First, scribbles on stones overshadowed pictorial writing on caves. As soon as humankind learned how to produce paper and better ink, scrolls quickly overcame stones. Then came the age of typewriters. Not even a century later, digital images and computer-based writing have become the fastest and easiest medium to share and store information.

Although it is remarkably revolutionary, the advent of digital currency represents just a fraction of the innovations the computer age has ushered in. While some schools of thought have said that digital currencies will not be sustainable in the long term, others have simply jumped on board the train to reap its existing advantages.

Many innovations have been successfully integrated into the modern world, so one cannot state that cryptocurrencies are completely unreliable. The world continues to evolve.

Time remains the only factor that can determine the boom or doom of any innovation.

CHAPTER 1: THE BASICS OF CRYPTOGRAPHIC CURRENCY

In basic terms, cryptocurrencies are virtual monies within a computer system. They are a series of digital records held by multiple parties, which track the amount of currency that individual wallets hold. A cryptocurrency can be said to be an asset which has been digitally designed to function as a medium of exchange. A cryptocurrency uses cryptography to protect and enhance transactions and to manage the inclusion of more units of that particular currency. Widely considered as alternatives to real currencies, cryptocurrencies are commonly referred to as digital currencies.

Matthew Field and Cara McGoogan, correspondents from the British newspaper The Telegraph, said that cryptocurrencies are types of private, virtual money intended to be adequately protected at all times. Cryptocurrencies are linked to the net and created using cryptographic processes. Their creation also involves the conversion of information into codes that are very difficult to crack, which essentially monitor their exchanges throughout the network.

Field and McGoogan said that originally, cryptographic procedures developed out of the need to protect the transmission of news and information during World War II. In the modern digital world, it metamorphosed into the foundation for the online distribution of private and protected information, with the help of advanced knowledge in computer science and more complex mathematical calculations.

Cryptocurrencies are usually referred to as "digital gold" because through preservation, they increase in value over time. As a medium of payment, cryptocurrencies are easy and convenient to use around the globe. Because transactions using cryptocurrencies are generally transparent, they also operate as a medium of payment in illegal transactions or activities.

Cryptocurrencies have given a massive kickstart to a new and rapidly growing marketplace. For instance, Poloniex (an exchange platform) has assisted in the trading of countless cryptocurrencies since they surfaced. Many of these exchange platforms experience larger percentages of trades than some European stock exchanges.

HAVE CRYPTOCURRENCIES LIVED UP TO THE HYPE?

One can say that a large percentage of the world's population is still very skeptical about the practicability of cryptocurrencies as a medium of economic exchange. However, the number of investors is increasing daily.

Many monetary policies put in place by governments have suffered setbacks due to cryptocurrencies because the latter are forms of money whose supplies are controlled and monitored without any interference from banks or financial institutions. Policies to manipulate inflation and deflation simply cannot work with cryptocurrencies.

A public speaker, Sarah Granger, once said that although cryptocurrencies are still not stable and are relatively new compared to gold, they are gaining ground and will likely undergo developmental tweaks in the near future. Granger said that cryptocurrencies became more popular in terms of awareness and acceptability as uncertainty plagued the post-election period. Granger also said that cryptocurrencies should be made easily available for adoption on a large scale, which would include the strengthening of security and safety provisions for investors and other users. In conclusion, Granger said that in a few years, the world will have advanced to a stage in which everyone is able to keep or hide their money with the help of cryptocurrencies, knowing that anywhere they go, their money will be within reach.

The invention of the first cryptocurrency, Bitcoin, marked a revolution in digital money, as early attempts to develop such technologies hadn't drawn much attention. Even Satoshi Nakamoto, the inventor of the blockchain on which Bitcoin thrives, did not envision the cryptocurrency's popularity. Bitcoin instantly caused a stir, and by the end of the first quarter of 2015 hundreds of cryptocurrencies were in existence.

A group of individuals–generally referred to as "miners"– balance ledgers, make modifications and are responsible for the general safekeeping of cryptocurrency platforms. Miners are experts who, using computers, timestamp as well as validate transactions by adding ledgers in a specific pattern to the system. These ledgers are assumed to be secure because of the belief that miners are financially motivated to keep the ledgers running.

Cryptocurrencies are essentially developed to reduce the manufacturing of national currencies. This, in turn, will limit the total value of currency in circulation. In 2008, Satoshi Nakamoto, the inventor of Bitcoin, was quoted as saying that his intentions were not to invent a currency. Instead, he had planned to develop a peer-to-peer electronic cash system.

Satoshi's invention was a breakthrough in the creation of digital money because he devised a way to build a decentralized digital system. Before him, there had been failed attempts to develop digital money. After observing the principal causes of these failures, Satoshi eliminated the idea of a centrally controlled system. Instead, he built a peer-to-peer network system. Decentralization caused the rise of cryptocurrency.

Digital cash was attained through a payment network with transactions and balances. However, a key issue that required resolution was the continuous stoppage of double spending. This was accomplished through a central server that contained all the balance details.

However, because a decentralized network has no central server, every entity on the network is responsible for storing and balancing records. Each peer has a record and a list containing all the transactions to ascertain the validity of future transactions.

In a decentralized network, the server is not present. Therefore, each entity in the network must do its part. Every peer in the network requires information about all of the transactions to determine whether all the forthcoming transactions are legitimate.

When peers encounter a dispute regarding a small balance, the transaction breaks down. A need exists for absolute agreement but the question remains: "How can a network without a central authority have a uniform agreement?"

No one could answer this question, and it appeared impossible to achieve. Satoshi eventually solved the problem. His solution was to obtain absolute agreement without the inclusion of a central authority. Eventually, the actualization of his aspirations played a major role in the success of digital currencies.

In 2009, Satoshi, who at the time was anonymous, created the premier decentralized cryptocurrency known as Bitcoin. It used a cryptographic hash function (SHA-256) as proof of its work scheme, which was based on the Tangle. Since then, many other cryptocurrencies have been introduced, but many have not been as successful as Bitcoin, as they offer little or no improvement in comparison. Curiosity about the Bitcoin phenomenon forced the treasury department in the UK to conduct a study on cryptocurrencies in 2014. The government wanted to know how cryptocurrencies could help develop the economy and whether appropriate regulations should be adopted with respect to their use.

STRONGHOLDS

An excerpt from Coin Pursuit states that virtual currencies such as Bitcoin are not governed by the rules and regulations of banks, financial institutions or governments. Digital currencies do not involve transaction fees or various other bank-related charges.

With respect to virtual coins, a "cold war" has been waged against fees, some of which are so effectively embedded that they cannot be confirmed. Additionally, in cases of inflation, national or government-supported currencies tend to lose their value. However, such situations do not necessarily diminish the value of digital currencies.

Due to their characteristics, cryptocurrencies have withstood criticisms. Some of these characteristics are:

UNIVERSALITY: The physical location of users or investors has no influence on transactions, as activities are linked globally through a network of computers on the internet. There is no need to physically meet any participant once a smooth flow of operations is established.

INSTANT TRANSACTIONS: In cryptocurrency deals, the initiation and confirmation of transactions is carried out almost instantly. Once every detail has been placed in the network, business is completed within seconds.

GUARANTEED SAFETY: Cryptocurrencies are securely stored using a cryptography system. This means that investors have unique private keys which serve as authentication for any transaction. The provision of constant random cryptographic numbers makes it impossible to steal or divert cryptocurrencies from users' accounts.

UNRESTRICTED ACCESS: Cryptocurrencies are readily available for anyone's use. No permission whatsoever is needed before transactions occur. Cryptocurrencies are accessible without restrictions.

ANONYMITY: Cryptocurrency accounts and transactions are not linked to real-life identities. The addresses shown during transactions are series of randomly generated characters which belong to other participants. While these addresses are used to monitor and analyze the flow of transactions, they do not necessarily correlate with the users' actual addresses.

THE EDGE OVER FIAT CURRENCIES

Some experts with the central bank have said that the consistent use of cryptocurrencies will reduce the bank's power to influence credit prices. According to these experts, the possibility also exists that a consumer's confidence in fiat currencies will drop significantly as cryptocurrencies gain more ground.

Banking officer Gareth Murphy said that agencies that compile statistical analyses of economies will experience great difficulty carrying out such tasks as cryptocurrencies become more popular. This would become a major challenge for governments, as such data is used to control their economies. Furthermore, Murphy warned that cryptocurrencies will reduce the central bank's grip on exchange rates and other money-related policies.

By 2016, almost all of the large accounting firms and popular computer science companies had researched cryptocurrencies and what could be gained from them. Publications and projects have sought to understand the full potential of cryptocurrencies.

At present, many have come to understand cryptocurrencies as milestone advancements in the finance sector. Already, governments, banks and financial institutions are aware of their importance.

Basel Ismail, a cryptocurrency geek, FinTech leader, Cornell MBA and Norwich InfoSec, said that the increased use of cryptocurrencies for commercial purposes, along with the introduction of other educational and developmental activities, can improve people's knowledge of the functions of a blockchain, the meaning of Bitcoin and the ways in which virtual tokens and currencies can assist individuals, thereby boosting the technology's popularity and polishing its image.

WHAT MINERS DO

Bob Mason (FX Empire) said that the cryptocurrency mining procedure is not the same as the mining procedure for valuables like silver and gold because the mining of cryptocurrencies doesn't yield physical assets. He said that while the mining of cryptocurrencies involves an electronic process and requires electronic wallets, commodity mining like that for gold usually involves searching for, digging up and excavating physical objects. However, the cryptocurrency mining process could, to an extent, be likened to investing in the future markets of valuables rather than currently visible ones.

Even if it is done through a cloud mining process from a service provider, through the purchasing of private mining software or through a data platform, the mining of cryptocurrency creates new sets of a digital currency in relation to the exact platform on which the procedure is being carried out. The mining process involves a lot of computation and becomes complex as its corresponding platform progresses. Some mining processes are already involved in finding solutions for cryptographic puzzles and consume lots of computer-related power.

Essentially, miners are experts within a cryptocurrency network and are responsible for the creation of currencies and the confirmation of transactions. To understand these tasks, a need exists to digest their databases' technicalities. Bitcoin, for instance, is a system of collaborators and records of all transactions kept by each collaborator. This ensures a balance of each account on the network or system. Simply put, when a file states that User A has given a certain amount of Bitcoin to User B, it gets signed by User A's private key. After the file has been authenticated, a transaction is directed from one peer to the other through a broadcast in the network. That is the basis of the peer-to-peer technology.

The entire network is instantly aware of this transaction. This is the stage at which miners play a crucial role, as the confirmation of such transactions would trigger the awareness.

It is important to note that confirmation is a crucial stage in cryptocurrency deals. In fact, cryptocurrencies thrive only on that basis. An unconfirmed transaction can be altered because it would still be on a pending list. However, once it gets confirmed, it cannot be reversed or tampered with. It instantly becomes a permanent record of the blockchain's transactions.

Miners are the only people who validate transactions. That's their primary responsibility in a cryptocurrency platform. They verify transactions by stamping and subsequently broadcasting them within the network. Once a miner confirms a transaction, all nodes must add it to their databases. It eventually becomes part of the blockchain. The miner receives tokens as a form of payment for their important role in the network. Interestingly, anyone can become a miner. The decentralized nature of the blockchain network makes it impossible to assign the mining tasks to specific sets of users. So that it can work for a long period, a cryptocurrency network cannot afford to restrict mining activities to a particular group, as this would increase the probability of abuse. The system would face destruction should a miner broadcast fake transactions across peers throughout the network. This is why Satoshi created a policy in which miners must find a way to connect new blocks with their predecessors through a cryptographic product referred to as a hash. This process is called Proof-of-Work. It has a hash algorithm of SHA 256. While it is not necessarily important to know all the technicalities of SHA 256, it is necessary to understand that it is more like a cryptologic puzzle from which miners constantly seek answers. Once the puzzle has been solved, a miner builds a block and adds it to the blockchain. The miner is then permitted to add a coinbase transaction, which ultimately earns the miner crypto cash.

To an extent, miners believe that mining is an interesting process which gives them the opportunity to acquire knowledge of complex electronic procedures.

Brian Roemmele, an alchemist and metaphysician, said that many of his friends in the technology sector already had knowledge of coding or ideas about the procedures and steps they were to follow. He said that currently it isn't easy to find individuals who understand what is happening with the hardware component for which they are writing codes. Roemmele mentioned that the mining process for algorithm-based currencies allows miners to realize the core importance of hardware components, which is enticing.

ACCEPTABILITY

As popular and successful as cryptocurrencies are, some countries have frowned at their use, while others have maximized their potential. The acceptability of cryptocurrencies in the economies of various countries varies depending on the situation. In Russia, for instance, citizens cannot purchase goods with any currency other than the ruble. However, cryptocurrencies are assumed to be legal. China has no tolerance for cryptocurrencies, which are illegal. Cryptocurrencies have also had differing receptions from firms and organizations not owned by the government. Issues of piracy and illegally acquired trademarks have stirred up controversies. The "Coinye" cryptocurrency is a famous example that got mixed up in lawsuit and was abandoned.

THE NECESSITY OF TIMESTAMPING

To eliminate the need for a third party to stamp all transactions added to the blockchain, cryptocurrencies use several schemes. The Proof-of-Work scheme was the first time-stamping scheme invented on the blockchain. However, the SHA 256-based hash is still the most-used Proof-of-Work algorithm. Through this scheme, Litecoin has confirmed more than 480 implementations on its network, giving it superiority in the cryptocurrency world.

Other algorithms common to the Proof-of-Work scheme include SHA-3, Blake and Crytonight, among others. Over the years, cryptocurrencies that use a combination of the Proof-of-Work and the Proof-of-Stake scheme have emerged. The Proof-of-Work scheme is the process of getting a cryptocurrency network and realizing general acceptance by asking users to prove they own a certain amount of money. Compared to the Proof-of-Work scheme, which runs somewhat complex algorithms to verify transactions, the Proof-of-Stake scheme depends on coins in particular.

MINOR SETBACKS

Since the invention of Bitcoin, other cryptocurrencies have essentially become replicas of it. The addition of a few tweaks sets them apart, but they cannot boast of cutting-edge advancements. To date, banking services do not include cryptocurrency trades and to a large extent, they decline contracts to help companies that deal with digital currencies. Another factor that scares off some enthusiasts is the probability of data loss. Malware could attack the database, destroy media and permanently remove cryptocurrencies from their networks.

To become mainstream, cryptocurrencies must achieve certain milestones. These milestones will become fast-tracked when the number of merchants trading with such cryptocurrencies increases. As technology continues to improve, the cost of the software and hardware that miners use increases. Furthermore, once several blocks confirm a transaction in a cryptocurrency platform, the process becomes irreversible.

A look at the living standards and resources available to the masses in remote countries around the world also highlights some disadvantages of digital currencies. A certain quality of internet connection is necessary for the production and flow of the currencies–a type of internet connection these areas don't have. A sufficient internet connection is very costly for many third-world residents, who lack fundamental infrastructure in their communications sector. However, as the internet continues to advance, one could guess that in 10 years these difficulties will have been resolved.

In addition, no "chargebacks"–used as a form of protection against fraud in credit card transactions–are available.

However, this feature is unnecessary in cryptocurrency platforms, as a third-party escrow equivalent to a "chargeback" can be used to conduct a transaction.

The amount of energy spent on mining cryptocurrencies has been a major concern of some environmentally conscious individuals. However, the energy usage is relatively small when compared to the energy consumed by traditional financial setups.

It is also important to note that a few multi-level marketing schemes have started due to the success of cryptocurrencies.

FINAL THOUGHTS

Ameer Rosic, a serial entrepreneur, investor, marketing strategist and blockchain enthusiast, once remarked that all things in the world would always have positive and negative sides. To choose the right things, individuals must consider the positive and negative sides very carefully. Ameer said that in dealings with cryptocurrencies, wide acceptability has more advantages than the technology behind the particular currency. The cryptocurrency's technology has arrived in full; only time will determine its acceptance by government bodies and private individuals.

With this concise background on the dynamics of cryptographic currency, the subsequent chapters will examine the most common types of cryptocurrencies in circulation.

CHAPTER 2: BITCOIN, ETHEREUM AND LITECOIN

Only a few other technological advancements can attract the interest of so many individuals online. The anxiety and enthusiasm surrounding Bitcoin can hardly be overshadowed by any other IT invention. Digital currency has been a source of curiosity since it entered the mainstream market approximately six years ago. Currently, interest in Bitcoin is at its highest level; its value has skyrocketed significantly, making millionaires out of those who previously acquired it in large quantities.

Bitcoin uses decentralized technology for smooth and safe payments and helps store money on its network without the need for real names. As advertised in the mass emails sent upon its introduction, Bitcoin was produced to liberate money in the same way the net provides free information to its users.

Paul Blough (BloughTech) said the acceptance and adoption of Bitcoin should not only be the subject of focus; rather, emphasis should be placed on the amount of time it will take other virtual currencies to use blockchain technology as well. He said that usually the earliest user of a type of technology is not its eventual leader. While development and research has focused on getting the best from blockchain technology, no specific standard has yet been set.

HOW BITCOIN IS WIRED

Like other prominent types of cryptocurrency, Bitcoin operates on a public ledger known as the blockchain.

"Bitcoin's P2P network architecture is much more than a topology choice. Bitcoin is a peer-to-peer digital cash system by design, and the network architecture is both a reflection and a foundation of that core characteristic. Decentralization

of control is a core design principle and that can only be achieved and maintained by a flat, decentralized P2P consensus network" – Andreas Antonopoulos

As mentioned earlier, the blockchain stores decentralized records of transactions held equally by every user of the network once they have been updated. Bitcoins are created when users manufacture blocks within the system. The computer abilities of users are used to cryptographically create every block. The block is then added to the blockchain, giving users the room to earn as well as the ability to keep the network in shape. To ensure its value keeps increasing, a restriction on the number of bitcoins that can be created has been embedded into the system. That said, the highest possible number of bitcoins that can be created is around 20 million. Currently, more than 14 million are in circulation.

UNMASKING THE BITCOIN INVENTOR

As mentioned earlier, Satoshi Nakamoto is the assumed pseudonym of the creator of Bitcoin and the blockchain in general. Numerous efforts to unveil the individuals behind this name have proven futile. Recently, a computer scientist from Australia was quoted as saying that he was Satoshi Nakamoto but he couldn't prove this claim. He subsequently confessed to having made this claim because he wanted the fuss about Satoshi's identity to die down.

THE POPULATION THAT HAS EMBRACED THE BITCOIN

Dieter Huelskamp said that with Bitcoin, there is no certainty regarding the number of Bitcoin users, as anyone can use multiple accounts for their exchanges. Also, some accounts can eventually be left idle permanently. However, Huelskamp suggested that one could trace some addresses that were used during transactions within the Bitcoin platform. Better still, one could check the number of addresses that had ever owned bitcoins. Huelskamp also said that the total number in 2014 was about 2.5 million. He said all of the information was embedded in the database and introduced during transactions. Another intriguing discovery was that many of the more than two million addresses had not been moved in about three years, which implied that users who are particularly active within the platform are largely minimal compared to those who use mostly fiat currencies.

Currently, about six million people around the world have procured cryptocurrencies. A large percentage of them have Bitcoin wallets. In recent times, renowned sites such as WordPress, Reddit, Namecheap and Mega have begun accepting payment in bitcoins for the services they provide.

BITCOIN'S ECONOMIC POWER

In response to a question about Bitcoin's economic implications, Pair (BitPay) said that Bitcoin users can transact internationally without any risk of fraud through credit cards or related electronic transactions. People occasionally overlook the fact that in some nations around the world, credit card payment is not possible. Such nations cannot participate in internet-based economic transactions. Therefore, if payment through Bitcoin becomes possible in such countries and if the United States government accepts the integration of this new and promising sector, the world's economy could receive a significant boost.

The transfer of monies without fees or charges, the investment of traditional currencies and the funding of companies' activities are among the most common uses of Bitcoin. Bitcoin can be used to purchase goods on some websites. Some stores in the UK also accept payments through Bitcoin. Sushi restaurants, pubs, CEX stores and Dell's website, among other vendors, are active traders of Bitcoin. Interestingly, there are several Bitcoin ATMs where bitcoins can be withdrawn. Other Bitcoin holders keep their bitcoins and hope that they will accumulate and earn a significant amount of interest. Electronics like cameras, computers, musical instruments and blood pressure monitors can be purchased at bitcoinstore.com, using bitcoins as the medium of exchange. There are also Bitcoin-friendly casinos, such as SatoshiBet. Bets of Bitcoin is another prediction market based mainly on bitcoins.

Generally, the infrastructure for administering the exchange and storage of bitcoins has grown rapidly. Exchange platforms, in-hand trade facilitators and Bitcoin debit card dealers have increased in number over the years.

Bitcoin wallets are essentially a set of specially designed programs that store users' bitcoins in the same way a regular wallet stores one's money. They can be judiciously used on a computer system or a standard smartphone. They can also be stored securely on the web so that they can be accessed from any corner of the world.

In addition, investors can safely keep their "paper wallets," as systems are available for their production and printing. There are equally advanced secure e-wallets for users who tend to misplace physical documents.

Casascius coins are already available for purchase. They are compilations and physical illustrations of most Bitcoin stories on the internet. Sold by Mike Caldwell on his website casascius.com, a casascius coin contains a private key on a particular card that has been embedded in the coin. These coins are then sealed with a hologram.

Mike Caldwell lives in Utah and owns a payroll software

business. He has about 30 employees and is not affiliated in any way with the Bitcoin Foundation. He is simply a highly informed and enthusiastic investor in the Bitcoin platform. He believes very strongly in a positive future for the Bitcoin market. He has been a long-time investor and has not stopped investing in the digital currency.

In an interview, Caldwell said that chaos and fear erupted when the crash occurred in 2011. He said that news spread that a site had been attacked, which led to assumptions that Bitcoin had failed as a cryptocurrency. Caldwell said that he purchased more coins while everyone else was in confusion.

Those who invested early in Bitcoin are now millionaires. Due to its volatile nature, the exchange rate can rise to unimaginable numbers within days. Since 2013 (the year in which Bitcoin became mainstream), the price of Bitcoin has gone up and down. In fact, that same year, its price rose about 10,000 percent. This trend didn't continue however, as the breakdown of MT Gox, the biggest Bitcoin exchange platform, caused its price to drop drastically. Soon after, the price began to rise once more and as of now, it is quite high. This success is attributed to the efforts of some regulators who constantly touted Bitcoin and trade tokens related to bitcoins. While some pundits have suggested that the recent rise in the price of bitcoins is just the beginning of greater exploits in the field, others believe it is just another period of rush susceptible to a crash.

The increase has also been linked to money laundering activities due to the inability to link a wallet to an individual.

INVESTING IN BITCOIN

Without a central server or a set of trusted parties, Bitcoin is decentralized. Every transaction is based on cryptographic proof and not on trust.

A note on Investopedia states that Bitcoin is very lucrative at the moment, with individuals, firms and institutions remaining in the system. For a regular individual, there are many ways to acquire and invest in Bitcoin. Sites such as Bitstamp, Local Bitcoin and Coinbase are well-known for their efforts to promote Bitcoin. Each site has advantages and disadvantages, so individuals should determine which is best for them.

With traditional currencies, a level of trust is required to make transactions work. For instance, customers must trust their banks to keep their money for them. They must be sure their money will be readily available for use at any point. Banks loan money in a bid to make a profit. However, with cryptographic proof in the digital currency system, there is no need for a third party or middleman. Transactions can be safe, fast and easy, and money can be stored properly.

Furthermore, the adoption of bitcoins is bound to increase with time. Its community is expanding rapidly. Chalmers Brown said that he believes if Bitcoin keeps increasing in popularity, with the inclusion of a stable price, additional organizations and individuals will start using it. Brown also said because efforts are being made to blend Bitcoin with the standards and regulations in many countries, and also because more research is being done to discover ways to use Bitcoin on the blockchain, users will eventually become more comfortable with it.

Through decentralization, Bitcoin has proven resistant to theft and fraud. Also, it charges no transaction fees. As the price increased from a few dollars to about $1,100 in 2013, Bitcoin was able to provide massive returns to its investors at the end of the same year. Those who invested more than $1,000 about five years ago are now millionaires.

It is important to note the volatility of bitcoin. In 2016, Bitcoin's price rose significantly. It even reached the inestimable height of $2,400. However, in May 2016 the price decreased to $400 in one day.

Nick Chandi, using the nickname SlickPie, has aired his views on the fact that cryptocurrency is here to stay even though mining has become relatively expensive. Perhaps investing in Bitcoin and other cryptocurrencies is still a good idea. He said that the Bitcoin evolution may be past its prime, as the digital currency world is still developing. The years during which the platform was similar to gold has passed. This enabled members of the mining pools to enjoy more of the currency because of the high number of investors who continued to use human and material resources as well as a significant number of technological products. Chandi concluded that this type of development would assist the growth of other cryptocurrencies.

THE MECHANISM OF MINING BITCOINS

The TV Tropes website said that Bitcoin is quickly being recognized by physical exchange stores and many merchants on the network. The site said it has started to function just like national currencies and continues to gain acceptance.

Mining bitcoins happens to be a very advanced technique. Graphic cards constitute one of several constraints and they cost about $500. In addition, expensive ASIC panels must be used to mine bitcoins for a while before any profit can be made. Miners have high electricity bills, which can be more than their gains from the mining procedures.

Another shortcoming in the process of mining Bitcoin is that an open-source computer program generates its rate according to a predetermined manner. This form of control was activated in 2009. The program has produced all of the 11 million bitcoins in circulation, and about 20,000 independent nodes run each bitcoin through a huge peer-to-peer network system. These nodes consist of very expensive G.P.U. or ASIC computer systems that are designed to compete for new bitcoins.

For every complex mathematical problem solved using a Proof-of-Work scheme, the Bitcoin platform releases a 25-coin reward to the fastest successful node in the network. Thereafter, the solution is spread throughout the network. This prompts a competition for a new block.

Initially, the Bitcoin software could be downloaded using any standard computer. Normal systems could run the program and even be used to mine bitcoins. Reaching a solution first was dependent largely on the amount of computer power users could dedicate to their calculations. This feature, however, strengthened the network as it created a computational race. Hence, more complex computing power allows achieving greater rewards just because of the additional power. Four years after the scheme started, purpose-built machines are the only systems with enough power to keep up with the existing nodes on the network.

The mining process makes the production of bitcoins anonymous in nature. Personally mined bitcoins are the most anonymous bitcoins on the entire system. Without any origin or history whatsoever, these bitcoins simply appear on the network.

Just as gold used to be mined, bitcoins are mined in small quantities as compared to the total supplies needed. This causes the supply to increase slowly. Twenty-one million coins have been newly injected into the Bitcoin software as the upper limit, and the last mining is predicted to occur in the year 2140. It has been predicted that by then, transaction fees will be in place to allow advancement rather than the mining of new coins. Currently, bitcoins are released first to miners, who then distribute them by buying goods or selling them to other ordinary investors who need digital currency.

Recently developed, custom-built Bitcoin-mining hardware and software is already available. This gives miners the opportunity to find bitcoins even faster than before. Every miner must solve a dual function as they process and secure transactions on the blockchain. It is important to note that the more miners who join the network, the harder it becomes to find bitcoins.

On all of the 20,000 network nodes within its system, the flow of ownership of every Bitcoin in circulation has been registered and validated with a timestamp. This authentication procedure helps eliminate double spending, as every coin exchange must pass through 20,000 separate observers. It is practically impossible to dupe all the network nodes at the same time without any suspicion. The technology is a formidable one indeed.

CONTROVERSIES

No doubt, the emergence of Bitcoin has marked a revolution in the cryptocurrency world as well as the finance sector. The milestone is not without its own controversies. Ben Lee of Neon Roots said that one doesn't have to look far for a reason behind Bitcoin's sudden recovery from the issues that plagued the platform at some point. He provided the example of China's economy.

He said, *"The SEC delayed their decision on the Winklevoss's Bitcoin exchange traded fund, which means we'll likely not see what happens for several more months under a new presidency."*

He concluded his argument by stating that government policies around the globe would not fund currencies with inadequate supplies. Some governments see Bitcoin as a threat to their national currency. Cristina Dolan of Trading Screen said that its volatile nature causes instability and sometimes panic.

She said that unlike what applies to traditional currencies and politics, the advancement of technology and some form of regulation continues to influence Bitcoin's volatility. Bitcoin's market capitalization reached 18 billion at the beginning of 2017. She said that the platform had 70 percent of trades as well as 90 percent of miners in China alone. Dolan believed that volatility would continue to cause problems for the cryptocurrency in the same year, as uncertainties still flooded economic and political policies.

While the future cannot be perfectly predicted, Bitcoin's success story can motivate individuals to keep investing. Gavin Andresen, an expert, said that he continues telling everyone that Bitcoin is still in an experimental phase. Money and time remain the best resources to invest in the platform. He said its volatility rate would determine its reliability and profitability in the long run, as it will take some time before it is fully trusted by everyone.

ETHEREUM (ETH)

Until now, to create blockchain applications, a complicated foundation in programming, cryptography and mathematics has been required. However, we have progressed from those times. Earlier applications that facilitated electronic voting, the transfer of properties and day trading can now be made and put into place faster than ever. Ethereum allows developers to create decentralized applications.

On its website, Blockgeeks said that in the past year Ethereum has been promoted to the forefront of the digital currency market. It bears some resemblance to Bitcoin in the way it is circulated. However, Ethereum has some very distinct features that set it apart from Bitcoin. The write-up said that Ethereum not only offers a reputable backing for Ether (its custom digital currency) but also has a distinct programs known as smart contracts.

Simply put, smart contracts are encoded computer programs that contain some form of transactional agreements. These sets of codes have been written to promptly execute the agreements for which they have been programmed, as soon as certain parameters are met. This is why Ethereum is referred to as "programmable money."

A UNIVERSAL COMPUTER SYSTEM

Essentially, the vision of the Ethereum cryptocurrency and its entire network is to build a worldwide community that further decentralizes the existing client-to-server networking model. Volunteers or enthusiasts can replace servers with what are known as "nodes" throughout the universe, forming a worldwide computer system in the process. Through this system, users from all parts of the world have equal opportunities to provide services within the network.

A typical explanation of Ethereum's vision is as follows. Today, Google has exclusive administrative power and control over all the apps in the Play store. Hence, users of theses apps sometimes cannot change them to suit their personal wants. However, Ethereum seeks to erase these kinds of administrative restrictions that are also initiated by third parties on the web. Instead, users have a form of individual control over their activities and the information they share on the network. Changes would be affected only by users who want to edit whatever they have included on the network.

While this vision appears possible due to the rate of technology advancement, presently, it is not possible to think of a particular blockchain that can carry out such a feat.

Ethereum, like other cryptocurrencies, has a system on which it thrives. The network requires "ether" to function. Ether is a programmable code issued as a reward for the provision of computational assets that are needed in the network. Ether can be likened to a bond in the digital form, which doesn't require the approval of third parties before it can be used. At its presale, 60, 102 and 216 Ether (ETH) were mined by many people.

THE ANNALS OF ETHEREUM

Ethereum was invented in 2013 by a Russian programmer named Vitalik Buterin. The altcoin was formally announced at the North American Bitcoin Conference that was held in the United States in January 2014. As said earlier, the vision was simply to achieve what Bitcoin couldn't. Ethereum was coded to process and execute DAO apps and smart contracts with no human interference.

In July 2014, the Ethereum foundation realized about $18 million from the presale of Ether tokens. This was after Dr. Gavin Wood joined the platform as a co-founder. From that moment on, interest in Ethereum has continued to grow. The introduction of the Distributed Autonomous Organization (DAO) into the network in April 2016 was Ethereum's turning point. It had the sole goal of creating a virtual community in which its investors could make decisions through smart contracts. The community would have no administrator or major influencer. It would simply run on coded rules and computer programming. The DAO enticed as many as 11,000 investors within a month and before the end of May 2016 a sum of $150 million had been invested into the program. That rate of investment is arguably one of the largest crowdfunding events in the modern world. Ethereum instantly became the digital currency everyone could bank on.

THE ETHEREUM BLOCKCHAIN

Henry Berg, an engineer, said that the Ethereum blockchain uses a distinct proof-of-work algorithm known as Ethhash. He also said that the platform accepts the execution of the Turing complete script. Those scripts that would willingly pay the charges for execution would be successfully processed on Ethereum. Henry said that things do not work that way in Bitcoin's network because it uses the SHA 256 algorithm for its proof of work. Also, Bitcoin does not support a large unit of script instruction.

The Ethereum blockchain is built using cryptographic mechanisms that make it resistant to alterations and hacking. It has a tamper-proof network which qualifies it as a formidable technology. It also boasts a decentralized pattern of operation within its network while blockchain synchronizes smoothly with Ether.

MINING OF ETHER

A new block is mined every 12 to 14 seconds. This equals a total production of 18 million ether yearly. Miners of ether are entitled to five ether each. On the Ethereum blockchain, ether is mined through the CPU and GPU mining processes using mining blocks.

THE ETHEREUM VIRTUAL MACHINE

The Ethereum Virtual Machine (EVM) is essentially the current-time setting for smart contracts within Ethereum. Because it is fully removed and sandboxed, the program working in the EVM cannot penetrate the network or its data processes. Each smart contract cannot even fully communicate with other smart contracts.

Contracts function on the blockchain based on an Ethereum-specific binary format (EVM bytecode). However, the contracts are usually inscribed in a complex Ethereum format, collected into byte code through an EVM compiler and then pushed on the blockchain using an Ethereum client.

THE ETHEREUM COMMUNITY

Thousands of computer systems simultaneously process every activity that occurs within the Ethereum blockchain. Also, smart contracts which have been written with programming codes are collated into "bytecode." The Ethereum virtual machine (EVM) then reads and processes the bytecode's contents. Other programming codes that could be written by Ethereum developers are Solidity and Serpent. This is important to note because these two languages are easier for users to read and write.

In the Ethereum network, all of the nodes process contracts through their Ethereum virtual machines. Also, as soon as a user takes an action within the network, all the nodes immediately reach a consensus before the transaction is processed. This is because each node has a copy of the transaction as well as a log of smart contracts in the network. Nodes are also responsible for monitoring the current condition of Ethereum's blockchain.

Although it might not be as useful as our modern-era web, if all of the plans and visions of the Ethereum community come to fruition, it would serve as a substitute for many sites everyone uses on daily basis. As long as users have ether, they should be able to access the platform, even from a simple smartphone.

THE EXPLOSIVE RELEVANCE OF SMART CONTRACTS

No doubt, the singular distinctive feature of the Ethereum cryptocurrency platform is the inclusion of smart contracts. Investopedia defines smart contracts as contracts that execute themselves according to the terms mutually agreed upon by the seller and the buyer. These agreements are transformed into codes and then distributed throughout the blockchain's decentralized network.

The smart contract program provides room for a trusted agreement or a transaction to be conducted between or among unknown participants with no administrative control, external regulatory actions or complex legal practices. Smart contracts make transactions transparent, irreversible and linkable.

Already many financial institutions agree that smart contracts would help greatly in facilitating settlements and performing quick transactions. Banks such as J.P. Morgan and Citibank have tried to process credit processes through smart contracts.

Furthermore, experts are beginning to realize that well-developed smart contracts can address some legal activities that would naturally require the services of a legal practitioner. Because they have been designed to operate strictly within specified rules known to both parties, the tendency for disputes would be reduced as stakeholders became aware of the consequences of a breach.

THE HACK

Soon after the launch of the DAO, hackers siphoned about $60 million in DAO tokens due to a loophole in the DAO program. As a measure to make the hack a futile one, developers on the Ethereum network launched the "Hard Fork," which expressly rendered the hacked transactions invalid. In the process, a new blockchain was developed. In addition, the Hard Fork was effected at the 192,000th block so as to repay lost tokens to their holders.

However, the protocol seemed to have demoralized some potential investors, whose concerns heightened regarding the security of their tokens. Just as a bank must go through the slow process of reform after fraud, miners and other stakeholders had to face the frustrating and gradual process of regulating the system back to its normal state.

Another crucial blow the hack dealt was the demolition of the principles of smart contracts. Smart contracts are programmed to be censorship-resistant but because the Hard Fork reversed all the activities within the Ethereum network, it immediately highlighted a backdoor to the resistant nature of the principles of smart contracts.

THE EMERGENCE OF ETHEREUM CLASSIC

As mentioned earlier, some users expressly frowned at the decision to introduce a Hard Fork into Ethereum's blockchain. These investors did not upgrade their version of the blockchain. They simply continued mining on the version before the hack. The 192,000th block where the Hard Fork was applied marks the point of difference between Ethereum's blockchain and that of Ethereum classic. However, the two platforms offer similar operations in terms of smart contracts and apps.

TOTAL MARKET VALUE

The total market value of Ethereum is currently $10 billion. This is less than half of Bitcoin's value, but it nevertheless represents a viable cryptocurrency. An ether (ETH) coin is worth about $126 and the value keeps increasing.

ETHEREUM WALLETS

With Ethereum, once a user loses their password, they permanently lose their ether. This is why one must have an Ethereum wallet. This necessity is a result of the absence of third parties in all transactions. Because no administrators control what users do, it is impossible to hold anyone responsible for a misplaced password or private key. A few types of wallets are available for the storage of cryptocurrencies on the web, and users can employ them to store their ether and passwords.

USABILITY OF ETHEREUM

On "quota", Admir Tulic, a cryptocurrency enthusiast who studied investing, said that although Bitcoin is a great product, it only has the singular function of acting as a currency. He said that the Proof of Work scheme wastes a lot of energy as well. If anyone wants to achieve more with a blockchain, they should support Ethereum instead. He said that Ethereum is a domain for multiple applications, such as crowdfunding, markets for predictions, gambling, the Internet of Things, the issuance of assets, domain registration and voting.

Already, there are many Ethereum-based applications and software. Some of these applications have already solved some basic modern-day difficulties, which are explained below.

Slock.it: The idea behind Slock.it is to create a world economy in which unused possessions can be freely shared or loaned to those who need them. These transactions, of course, would be backed by smart contracts, eliminating the tendency of a breach. According to research, more than 60 percent of the world's population is willing to exchange their possessions for monetary gains. Slock.it is trying to make that desire a reality.

Ether Tweet: Eth-tweet is another application currently run within the Ethereum platform. It is a mini-blog which operates like Twitter. Eth-tweet allows users to share content in a decentralized way. In essence, what users upload or distribute does not encounter any form of censorship. The Ethereum blockchain simply lets its activities run smoothly without a third party's intervention. On the platform, users' up-voted content receives ether.

Uport: This platform offers to develop a unified identity database for everyone around the world. It places organizations and customers on a common ground where all parties' true identities are known. Its use of smart contracts also means that transactions are completed easily and on time. Identities are verified upon the delivery of products or services.

Golem: This is an open-source computer whose computational power is realized from elaborate data centers as well as personal computer systems. Any user within the platform can use Golem's resources to carry out difficult computation tasks and access websites seamlessly. With the application, users can also mine cryptocurrencies.

DIFFERENCES BETWEEN BITCOIN AND ETHEREUM

Because it was the first form of cryptocurrency to be mined, Bitcoin will continue serving as the source of comparison with other cryptocurrencies. In this case, however, the platforms have several important differences. By extension, Ethereum preserves programming logic even though its blockchain handles decentralized transactions as well. The Ethereum network saves transactions' procedures permanently for future reference. Also, Bitcoin doesn't use smart contracts, while Ethereum transactions are always backed up by smart contracts.

These notable differences do not necessarily make Bitcoin and Ethereum competitors. The two cryptocurrency platforms are constantly trying to create a brighter future by addressing the financial, social and technological constraints that plague the modern world.

Ameer Rosic, an entrepreneur, marketing nerd, investor and blockchain preacher, said that although many people try to compare the features of Bitcoin and Ethereum, the two platforms are in fact different in structure and mission. Bitcoin has proven itself to be a reliable virtual currency but Ethereum has the goal of achieving additional feats. Furthermore, it is important to note that ether is just one part of the Ethereum-based smart contracts program.

ETHEREUM'S FUTURE

In addition to monetary values, the evolution and advancement of smart contracts and DApps promises to be a liberating one.

A prominent cryptocurrency investor, Niels Soete, made some bold remarks concerning Ethereum's prospects. He said, "Ethereum has great potential and I see it reaching $500 this year and even go higher in 2–3 years! ($125 on the 20th of May 2017). Just buy some Ethereum, lock them up and look at it in 1 year, it will be one of the best investments you have ever made. A lot of great things are coming up for Ethereum. They have a great network coming up with DApps (decentralized apps). Their technology is just too good to not break through. While Bitcoin is already outdated, this is just the beginning for Ethereum. One day Ethereum will overtake Bitcoin as the biggest cryptocurrency and it will be sooner than you think."

Who knows? This might be the beginning of something even greater than the internet.

The Ethereum blockchain continues to improve through the introduction of problem-solving platforms. The innovations will not stop. More thirlling features are already on their way and the world anxiously awaits them.

LITECOIN (LTC)

As specified earlier, Bitcoin might be the godfather of cryptocurrencies but there are hundreds of altcoins (or alternative cryptocurrencies) other than Bitcoin. Each cryptocurrency has tried to create its own technology and mission to change the face of the world economy. One of those alternatives is Litecoin.

"With substantial industry support, trade volume, and liquidity, Litecoin is a proven medium of commerce complementary to Bitcoin" – Litecoin wiki

Litecoin is the second cryptocurrency that hit the digital financial world after the emergence of Bitcoin. It also exists on the internet as "digital currency," which means it can be neither felt, touched nor minted. Although it has some basic similarities to Bitcoin, Litecoin is based on an entirely different protocol. It is a peer-to-peer cryptocurrency that can be used to make instant payments to different parts of the world without any cost. Litecoin is equally enforced with strong cryptographic calculations to ensure secure transactions. Its platform is a decentralized and open source network like many others.

As in other digital currencies, Litecoin does not originate from the government. Without governmental regulation or publication at a government control bureau, Litecoin's coins are generated through a sophisticated process of mining. This also includes the filing of some lists of transactions in the platform.

REASONS FOR LITECOIN'S INVENTION

On the 7th of October 2011, Charlie Lee, a former Google employee, introduced Litecoin to the internet world through the website GitHub. Litecoin's invention was intended to complement or update Bitcoin's glitches. Issues such as the timing of transactions and concentrated mining pools likely motivated Lee to create another cryptocurrency which would eliminate such difficulties. Litecoin was developed from some of Bitcoin's core codes but a few recognizable modifications were included to boost Litecoin's chances of acceptance on the web. From the 10-minute confirmation timing on the Bitcoin platform, Lee could reduce the confirmation timing of blocks to two-and-a-half minutes on the Litecoin platform to ensure that more transactions could be conducted and confirmed within a short period of time. At that rate, the transaction speed was about four times faster than that of Bitcoin transactions. Instead of the SHA-256 algorithm dominantly used in Bitcoin, the scrypt algorithm was introduced to Litecoin.

The scrypt algorithm upgraded the concentrated mining pool found in Bitcoin. The rate at which it consumes memory doesn't encourage concentrated mining pools. More details on the scrypt algorithm will be discussed later. Other noteworthy advancements include the introduction of Segregated Witness (SegWit) as well as the Lightning Network. These two introductions helped reduce the traffic jams which sometimes occur on the Bitcoin network. An increased number of transactions is conducted smoothly within a specific period of time.

LITECOIN'S CORE DEVELOPERS

Five years after it became mainstream, Warren Togami and Charlie Lee were the only known administrators associated with Litecoin. During that time, Togami was the principal developer.

However, another developer surfaced in 2016 under the pseudonym "Shaolinfry." Currently, other participants monitor updates and new releases. They also ensure the smooth running of all activities on the platform. The official acronym for Litecoin is LTC.

In November 2013, the 0.8.5.1 version of the Litecoin network was launched on the internet. That version had a better security gateway, thereby reducing the software's vulnerability. Soon after, in December of the same year, another version (0.8.6.1) of the Litecoin network was released. Binaries and the source code were quickly given to users in the IRC channel for Litecoin, on Reddit and on the official Litecoin forum. Transaction fees were reduced significantly as well. The release acknowledged that the main website would be updated as soon as several participants had begun running the version. More importantly, miners were given the room to include a "supernode" update on their configurations on the platform.

The update ensured that investors who had the software's older version would also benefit from the decreased charge for transactions within the network. The most recent upgrade is the 0.8.7.1 version, released in April 2014. In this version, Litecoin developers fixed the "Heartbleed" security issues.

WHAT IS THE TOTAL NUMBER OF LITECOINS?

Because Litecoin transactions occur at a rate four times faster than those of Bitcoin, Litecoin's developers have estimated that 84 million Litecoins are set to be mined. This could increase the chances of some blocks being left out of the process; however, a double spending incident is far less probable in Litecoin.

Fifty-one million Litecoins have already been mined and are currently in circulation while about 33 million more are set to be mined.

Arithmetically, a total of 14,400 Litecoins are produced daily, as 25 coins are generated every two-and-a-half minutes of a block. Therefore, by 2020, about three-quarters of all possible Litecoins will have been mined and placed into circulation. These mined Litecoins are the rewards for miners, who then sell them to the public in exchange for other monies.

THE VALUE OF LITECOIN

In cryptocurrency markets, the current market capitalization of Litecoin is close to one million dollars. This is because a single unit of Litecoin already costs as much as $45 or more. This increased rate has made Litecoin one of the most popular cryptocurrencies on the market. In addition, if a certain equal number of bitcoins and Litecoins were destroyed because some investors on the two platforms lost their private keys, the purchasing power of Litecoins automatically becomes larger than that of bitcoins once one Litecoin is valued at being more than 0.25 bitcoins. Although the aforementioned analysis is an assumption, one cannot rule out its possibility.

PURCHASING LITECOINS (WEBSITES AND EXCHANGE PLATFORMS)

If one's country is supported in the database, the Coinbase website is one of the easiest places through which Litecoin can be purchased. You just register an account with the website, synchronize your bank account and exchange the national currency that has been deposited into Coinbase's wallet for Litecoin. Other websites on which Litecoins can be acquired are BitStamp, Changelly and Shapeshift.

LITECOIN'S MINING PROCEDURES

The actual intention for using the scrypt algorithm was to ensure that Litecoins could be mined alongside Bitcoin.

Additionally, its adoption creates equal opportunities for GPU, ASIC, FPGA and CPU miners. The SHA-256 algorithm used in Bitcoin makes the mining process a very parallel one. Apart from the scrypt algorithms' dependence on large memory capacities and instant mathematical calculations, it uses the SHA 256 hash as an additional part of its program. This way, difficulty is encountered when one runs scrypt algorithms in a parallel form with the use of standard graphics cards. Another implication is that the SHA 256 ASIC hardware is not as costly as the scrypt's ASIC hardware. Litecoin mining has also benefitted from recent GPUs due to the large size of their RAM. However, Bitcoin mining benefitted more from CPU advancements in comparison to Litecoin.

Furthermore, Litecoin uses parameters (N=1024, p=1, r=1) which, to an extent, give room to normal users, who process and verify blocks to run many operations simultaneously without a lag in the proceedings. Usually, an enthusiast with an internet-enabled computer system can mine Litecoins right away. This situation is essential for maintaining the continued productivity of the Litecoin network. Thus, the participation costs are generally low. An important advantage of this cost-effectiveness is that decentralization within the system increases. Although they are not as effective as standard GPUs, CPUs can be used in the Litecoin mining process. Miners' reward for each block is 50 Litecoins.

The following is a detailed explanation of Litecoin's mining process, provided by an expert.

"For a miner to mine Litecoins with the use of their CPU, he or she should double click directly on the file "MineWithCPU.bat" from a folder named, 'Mine Litecoins with CPU.' As long as the user's hardware can handle it, their computer will start to mine Litecoins. And for a test worker, a setup has been programmed at the mining pool called POOL-X. However, several minutes might pass before such a miner would get a share. The process of mining Litecoins with one's CPU is not so resourceful but the user would experience the way it operates by processing this aforementioned file."

"But if a miner is to mine Litecoins through their GPU, he or he must double click on the file, 'MineWithAMDGPU.bat' from a folder named, 'Mine Litecoins with GPU/AMD' as long as such miner's graphic card has been produced by AMD (Ati). However, if the graphics card was produced by Nvidia, the user needs to double click on the file 'MineWithNvidiaGPU.bat' from a folder named, 'Mine Litecoins with GPU/Nvidia.' If the user's hardware can successfully process it, as well as [if] the miner that has been integrated identifies the graphics card on the user's computer correctly, mining Litecoins will subsequently begin. Also, for other test workers using GPUs, the mining POOL-X would have to be set up but it would definitely take many minutes before the users would be able to get their share as well. These days, it is best for miners to mine Litecoins through the use of their GPUs. Already, the platform has users who possess many graphic cards which have been set up for the mining of Litecoins at the same period of time; therefore, it might take new miners many days before they get to a whole Litecoin using just one GPU. Altogether, users can get an idea [about] the way in which GPU mining operates on a graphics card through the launch of the aforementioned file(s)."

The expert further said:

"Now that you have tested your hardware and know you can mine Litecoins correctly, you may join a mining pool and change the name of my workers and the URL of POOL-X which you can see if you edit the files 'MineWithCPU.bat' and 'MineWith (AMD/Nvidia) GPU.bat.' Write instead the names of the workers you created on your pool of choice and its URL:port, so you can mine Litecoins for yourself (this URL:

port information is given to you when you make an account on a mining pool). If you don't know how to join a mining pool then this may be a problem." (Weusecoins.com)

If a miner wants to mine Litecoins independently under the assumption that the user has standard and comprehensive hardware, the user is advised to complete the following processes.

"At first, the miner has to copy the file, 'litecoin.conf' provided in a free package that is available online, to their existing Litecoin directory which in most cases is: 'C:\Users\YOURNAME\AppData\Roaming\Litecoin'). Then, the user would find their way to the directory in which Litecoin application had been installed. It would probably be installed in: 'C:\Program Files (x86)\ Litecoin \'); the user should then launch 'litecoin-qt.exe' and exercise patience until he or she has been fully integrated to the network."

Afterwards, the user is expected to launch the file "SoloMineWithCPU.bat", which is in a folder named "Mine Litecoins with CPU", or the file "SoloMineWith (AMD/Nvidia) GPU.bat", which is in a folder named "Mine Litecoins with GPU/ (AMD/Nvidia)". Also, the two can be launched simultaneously. The user's computer components will then start to mine Litecoins. Sometimes, the user spends a significant amount of time discovering a full block. However, a miner can also sometimes be very lucky and discover a full block within a minute. Who knows what will happen?

The expert also said there are two things to note. The first is: *"the online miner that he has personally provided for CPU mining is Pooler's CPU miner 2.3.2, the one for AMD GPU mining is CGMiner 3.7.2 and the one for Nvidia GPU mining is CudaMiner-2013-11-15."* (Source: Weusecoins.com)

He mentioned that many other type types of miners might work more suitably for users' hardware, thereby enhancing the speed of the mining process.

The second observation is that some strict antivirus programs see all cryptocurrencies as malware. The expert said a lingering issue is that some dishonest users keep them in other legal packs of software to ensure those set of users mine in their stead on some systems while their owners are completely unaware. He also said that when they were eventually discovered, some companies that produce antiviruses tagged them as being a threat to computer systems.

ADDITIONAL BENEFITS

While Bitcoin can be costly due to the massive investment required for its mining, Litecoin's scrypt algorithm ensures that a large memory capacity is required for every hash process. This makes it extremely costly to invest a lot at once in Litecoin mining.

Another milestone achievement with Litecoin is the possibility for miners to be embedded on sites. Other visitors can add value to the websites through the simultaneous disposition of CPUs as they browse.

BLOCKCHAIN

The continuous and rapid production of blocks within the Litecoin blockchain causes it to coordinate and facilitate more transactions than does the Bitcoin blockchain. There is also no need to brush up the Litecoin blockchain in the coming years. Because of this advancement, investors have ample time to await confirmations and transact more often.

WALLET ENCRYPTION

Adequate cross checking and protection from malware that wipes out wallets is one of the advantages of the encrypted wallets found in the Litecoin network. Litecoin wallets are programmed in such way that users can expressly access their account balances and monitor transactions. In addition to the existing modes of security checks, users must provide personal passwords before they can use Litecoins to make purchases.

MAINTENANCE OF A SMALL MINING POOL

Because a miner gets more Litecoin rewards in a fewer number of minutes and with lesser variance than the miner would experience in Bitcoin, it becomes easier to maintain a small mining pool in the network. Hence, decentralization of activities increases. Investors ultimately become anxious to receive confirmation of their transactions within a few minutes. Litecoin merchants certainly get more coins than their Bitcoin counterparts in the same number of minutes.

MINING DIFFICULTY

In cryptocurrency, difficulty is the rate of difficulty one encounters in finding a new block. Generally, difficulty changes after 2,016 blocks in Bitcoin and Litecoin, but due to the time frame required to confirm transactions on the Litecoin network, difficulty usually arises after three-and-a-half days. The speed at which difficulty resurfaces on the Litecoin network addresses instances in which the network's computation power drops significantly due to miners' uninformed opt-outs.

CONCLUSION

Litecoin's reflection of Bitcoin's minor technical glitches has not made it as valuable as Bitcoin. However, since its introduction, it has not only proven easier to obtain, but also has seamless and faster transactions. In addition, Litecoin offers improved security measures, while the inclusion of both CPU and GPU mining techniques creates no significant constraints with respect to participating in the Litecoin network. Its value in the years to come might soar even more.

A comparison of Litecoin and Bitcoin's history and development vividly shows that Litecoin has gone further when it comes to blending with the latest developmental programs and software. For example, the Segregated Witness program has been launched in Litecoin's platform with no glitches. Even the original developer, Charlee Lee, is back with the Litecoin Foundation after spending some time with Coinbase. Also, the Litecoin team has begun working on new developments, such as integrating smart contracts and introducing the Lightning network. As soon as the new features have been fully launched, the future of Litecoin, as well as that of cryptocurrencies in general will brighten.

CHAPTER 3: RIPPLE (XRP)

The Ripple cryptocurrency is based on an open-source internet protocol and a consensus database. It is also known as the Ripple Transaction Protocol (RTXP). Its currency is referred to as XRP. Ripple is a currency exchange and effective settlement platform whose success can be attributed to its instant, secure and almost feeless conduct of transactions within its system.

Essentially, Ripple doesn't support any form of chargeback. Tokens in the form of cryptocurrencies, fiat currencies and other valuable commodities can be used for transactions within the Ripple platform. Using the yardstick of its market capitalization, Ripple comes just after the Bitcoin and Ethereum cryptocurrencies. Since its introduction, multiple payment platforms and even some banks have used Ripple's technology.

Nathan Ihara, a prominent freelancer who has worked with Ripple developers, said he can emphatically state that the Ripple cryptocurrency blends better with any sector other than Bitcoin. Its functions and application also cover a wider scope than Bitcoin does. Ihara said there is no doubt that Bitcoin created a globally recognized revolution in cryptocurrency, which can be termed "digital gold." However, Ripple seeks to help individuals as well as corporate organizations that are not concerned with digital currencies or gold.

Ihara cited an example. He said that if a non-profit organization began using Ripple to facilitate easy contributions to India, contributors would cut down on fees that could have been in the billions of dollars. Ihara also said that if a United States payment platform began using Ripple to enhance micro payments, it would be good development as well because users could give a website funds as low as 0.01 dollars. Then, as an add-on, all those who signed up for the micro payment would be able to transfer money to India.

Furthermore, Ihara suggested that all users didn't have to maintain an interest in decentralized currencies or even know about Ripple. All they had to know was that payments would become cheaper and easier. Also, he said that as the network continues to grow, so too would its advantages and features.

Ihara said that competition that pressurizes the "walled garden" monetary platform might yield significant changes. When he considered his own personal contribution, he found the platform's transaction processes to be the most thrilling aspect since they were simple and had basic features. The platform ensures a glitch-free and decentralized ledger on the network.

Ihara also said that when one thinks about the platform, one will realize that it has created room for more remarkable innovations that help traditional money users as well as cryptocurrency enthusiasts in general. If users begin using and gaining more knowledge of the network after the source has been launched, the similarities between Bitcoin and Ripple will become easier to identify.

THE ANNALS OF RIPPLE AND ITS GRADUAL DEVELOPMENT

After working with an exchange system in Vancouver, Ryan Fugger introduced Rippleplay to the Internet in 2004. He was a programmer whose initial desire was to invent a decentralized platform or community where participants could generate their own currency. Fugger's desire in the early stages saw him develop rippleplay.com. The website was designed to function as a secure online payment platform for transactions around the world. However, after McCaleb and Larsen convinced Fugger to implement a new and advanced function into his program, he made room for tweaks. Along with the two programmers, he founded the Opencoin Corporation in 2012.

The Ripple Transaction Protocol (RTXP) became the first payment network to be developed through Fugger's recommendations. RTXP facilitates instant money transfers from two users. Therefore, the need for a third party (as experienced in the traditional banking system) was eliminated. In addition, service fees and waiting periods were completely left out of transactions within the network. At a certain point, all popular currencies could be traded on the platform. Ripple is structured to depend on a ledger whose transaction records are constantly compared by independent servers. Afterwards, Opencoin invented its custom currency that was named XRP. It is a virtual currency which functions like Bitcoin. In the process, Ripple announced its cooperation with Bitcoin by introducing the Bitcoin Bridge. The development created room for Ripple users to use any currency to make payments to a Bitcoin address.

Ripple Labs Inc. became the new company name in September 2013, and it remained the main producer of programmed codes to the Ripple-based consensus and verification system. Subsequently, Ripple forged a partnership agreement with ZipZap, which ultimately led to a controversy with respect to Western Union.

INTEREST IN THE BANKING SECTOR

Many developmental projects arose in 2014. One of them was the creation of Android- and IOS-based applications for the transfer and reception of money (although use of this application has since been halted). Subsequently, "Codius" was introduced into the system. According to Larsen, Ripple's CEO, Codius's primary use was to facilitate payments through smart contract systems that did not require central operators. Since 2013, more banks and financial institutions have continued to use Ripple's protocol, which essentially allows customers to make payments throughout different countries. Officially, the first bank to use this protocol was Fidor Bank in Munich, Germany. Between 2015 and 2016, Ripple launched a branch in Australia, marking a major development point for the organization. Many other branches were opened across Europe and more institutions announced their partnership with Ripple. Ripple officially became the fourth company with a BitLicense in June 2016 after it obtained a license for its virtual currency from the New York State Department of Financial Services.

Addressing its interest in the banking sector and financial institutions in general, an article on Ripple's website said that in an era when bank-to-bank settlements reign, Ripple creates an unexpected worldwide connectivity and reduced transaction costs, which makes corporate disbursements and retail transactions very lucrative.

The currency's protocol is unique when compared to those of Ether and Bitcoin due to its quick and seamless transactions and decentralized governance. When dealing with this cryptocurrency, banks can save more than 60 percent of their costs.

MECHANISMS

Due to its open source mechanism, an existing peer-to-peer structure enhances the transfer of valuables between parties. Hence, differences in borders, currencies or networks do not hinder the remittance or transfer of currencies. The excerpt below sheds more light on this matter.

"In many ways, Ripple actually represents a new and improved version of Bitcoin and an evolution in blockchain technology. Ripple improves existing financial infrastructures with almost real-time transaction settlements- it is also

currency/value agnostic and is built to be compliant with existing financial laws and regulatory frameworks," – Ryan Charleston, marketing and business development professional.

Bitcoin can maintain its value within the cryptocurrency world. However, Ripple offers more effective transaction procedures and a comprehensive system of circulating digital value across different parts of our world.

Hence, using cryptographically structured transactions, Ripple users can transfer and make payments seamlessly with either fiat currencies or XRP, the platform's custom-made digital currency. While transactions conducted with other denominations reflect only debts, transactions conducted with Ripple's own currency are adequately documented in its ledger. To foster trust among its participants, Ripple has created security checks and validations for all its services. Payments are now made through a string of trusted parties in a process known as "rippling."

THE ARCHITECTURE OF RIPPLE'S PROTOCOL

Payment Gateways: This is a platform which lets Ripple users transfer and withdraw funds from Ripple's pool. A gateway provides balances and documents credits from users into Ripple's ledger.

Essentially, a gateway functions like a bank while using Ripple's protocol. At some point, Ripple's gateway may instruct users to provide some sort of verification with personal documents such as their addresses or nationalities, as is seen in AML and KYC policies. This is done to eliminate the possibility of scams and other illegalities. Popular gateways on the platform include Mr. Ripple, Ripple Fox, the Rock Trading, RippleChina and so on.

Ripple's chief cryptographer, David Schwartz, said that

payment mediums in the modern era can be likened to the position "email" was in decades ago. Schwartz said that all providers created personal platforms for their users and because users used distinct platforms, they could not communicate with one another. However, Ripple was created to combine many payment platforms in its network.

Initiation of Rippling and Trustlines: When a Ripple user can bear the risks involved in a gateway, a trustline is created manually. This means that users must have a level of trust in the Ripple's gateway's ability to keep and record their deposits. However, this trust must be regulated by including a limit on the trust levels as well as a limit on currency deposits on the user's gateway.

Furthermore, an option (rippling) permits a user's balance to switch between gateways if the user has multiple gateways in the same currency denomination. Users ultimately receive some form of meagre reward for transacting through multiple gateways.

Medium of Payment and Forex System: Within three to five seconds, deals and intra-currency transactions are conducted with Ripple. Because its verification process is cryptographic and algorithmic, transactions are fast, accurate and efficient. Also, payments are validated without any form of intermediaries or third-party witnesses, giving account holders the exclusive ability to activate and process transactions. Ripple also ensures that balances after transactions are almost instantly available with the provision of proper notifications to its users.

Ripple's other distinctive features include an irreversibility of payments and transactions in general and an absence of chargebacks. No one can seize or inactivate XRP. An update to the system in 2015 required new users to provide basic identification details before they could sign up.

Ripple's Bitcoin Bridge: Essentially, the Bitcoin Bridge allows users to make Bitcoin payments through their Ripple accounts. It serves as a link between the two platforms. With the Bridge, users can send bitcoins directly from Ripple wallets without visiting the central exchange platform (BTC-e). Other integrated exchanges, such as Bitstamp, can expressly complete such transactions.

Private Transactions: In the Ripple platform, it is extremely difficult and somewhat impossible to trace transactions to a specific user or institution. While Ripple's ledger is a publicly distributed one, its payment details are not.

Ripple's Market Makers: Providing services like market liquidity, rippling and multiple gateway conversions automatically qualifies any user as a market maker. Trading desks can also be deemed market makers. With an adequate population of market makers within the system, a smooth market which enhances users' ability to pay each other through the network is achieved. The freights of foreign exchanges are eliminated in the process.

In addition, users can easily convert currencies with market makers. They can also transfer funds using a different currency from that which the recipient would eventually receive. For instance, a recipient can choose to receive in bitcoins a sum of money paid in dollars.

The Open API Network: Ripple's payment network is based on the REST API standard, which helps make the system's protocol a user-friendly and easily accessible one. However, the payment network was extended to Magneto, an e-commerce platform that helps create payment invoices from Ripple's public ledger. Currently, Ripple has a payment wallet optimized for retail transactions.

XRP: This is the native virtual currency within Ripple's network. It is represented using six decimal positions, with the least position divided into what is known as a Drop.

Being the sixth place, a million drop is equal to 1XRP. When Ripple was introduced, a total of 100 billion XRPs had been pre-mined, implying that this is the amount of Ripple that would ever be in circulation, as the protocol in which Ripple operates would not permit further productions. This has increased the scarcity of XRP, causing a gradual reduction in its supply. XRP remains the only currency within the network that isn't prone to a counterparty risk. Although XRP doesn't have to be used for exchanges or the storage of values, every Ripple user must have about 20XRP in their account. The reasons for this limited amount of XRP were highlighted in the section about Ripple's website.

IDEOLOGY

Circulation: Ripple developers retained 20 billion XRP from the 100 billion that had been created. The remaining 80 billion were given to Ripple Labs to strengthen XRP's value and liquidity. The continued scarcity of XRP forced Ripple developers to inject 55 billion XRP into an escrow which is supposedly secured cryptographically. The escrow allows for sales of up to one billion XRP monthly and retrieves unused XRP to its queue. This particular process is repeated every month. The Ripple charts website regularly shows the XRP distribution and circulation rates.

Ripple as an Alternative Currency: An important functionality of XRP is its ability to substitute for other currencies should they not be available for exchange at some point in the platform. XRPs are transferred freely against some currencies within Ripple's network, which causes its fluctuation against such currencies. To make certain transactions easier for market makers who find themselves transacting with scarce currencies, Ripple launched a feature called "autobridging." By extension, autobridging helps improve a system's liquidity rate.

Transaction Fees as a Security Measure/Technique: Ripple deducts a transaction fee whenever users transact with currencies other than XRP. The fee ensures that the network is not flooded and that hackers find it extremely difficult and expensive to create fake accounts, distribute fake currencies and transact illegally within the platform. Such occurrences could have major consequences on the system's easy and quick transaction processes, as the network would automatically be overloaded. Thus, the 20 XRP in every legitimate user's account becomes useful. At a minimum, the transaction charge is 0.00001XRP for a single transaction. However, this fee doesn't go into any wallet or store. It is automatically erased from the system once the transaction is complete. This process is known as burning.

ACCEPTABILITY

Due to constant media coverage and the fact that several financial institutions have adopted it, the Ripple protocol has achieved a good measure of relevance and popularity. Its heightened security measures, which other cryptocurrencies like Bitcoin lack, give it an advantage. It's not surprising that an article in The New York Times described Ripple's increasing popularity as: "Winning something that has proved elusive for virtual currencies." Ripple continues to be an efficient medium for transacting across different continents and among diverse institutions. Ripple received the Technology Pioneer award from the World Economic Forum in August 2015.

COMPARISONS TO OTHER DIGITAL CURRENCIES.

Ripple remains third in the cryptocurrency world (after Bitcoin and Ethereum) in terms of market capitalization. However, several experts believe it is a viable alternative to Bitcoin due to its perfectly timed money transfers across different countries.

Any type of asset can be integrated into Ripple's network. It is so comprehensive that if a user wants to send US dollars but the recipient wants to receive this amount in a different national currency, Ripple's network can take care of the matter easily. Such actions are very difficult to process in Bitcoin's network. However, that does not make Ripple an immediate competitor of Bitcoin. The two platforms have exclusive functions unique to themselves and can coexist.

REACTIONS TO XRP

Critics and Bitcoin faithfuls have continually brought up controversies related to Ripple, such as its pre-mined currency and its developers' unnecessary hoarding of 20 percent of the 100 billion XRP. However, such controversies have died down since McCaleb and Arthur Britto decided that their XRPs would be sold. Chris Larsen also contributed seven billion XRP to the Ripple foundation, and by 2016 about 10 percent of the initially hoarded 20 percent had been given to charities and non-profit organizations.

Ari Levy, a senior tech reporter with CNBC, said that XRP has continued to exist comfortably with Ether, Bitcoin and other virtual currencies like Monero and Dash. He said that all these currencies are gaining from the increased use of blockchain. However, in contrast to many other cryptocurrencies, Ripple is owned, maintained and developed by a particular organization.

Levy said that this characteristic of Ripple has led to complaints from its users as well as those who are considering investing in it. They rear that Ripple's administrators may take advantage of the policy. He said, *"That's led to concern among XRP investors and enthusiasts that Ripple will one day decide to capitalize on its massive stake and flood the market with currency. Some venture investors would surely welcome cashing in on some of that value after pouring about $94 million into the company."*

Levy also said that participants who have thousands or even millions of dollars stored in XRP are particularly unsettled due to the fear of an unexpected rush of supply, especially considering the volatile nature of digital currencies.

CHAPTER 4: THE DASH CRYPTOCURRENCY

Decentralization has been key to the evolution of cryptocurrencies. However, investors have expressed interest in more avenues to keep these decentralized transactions private and by extension, to maintain anonymity. Bitcoin's inability to provide this service led to the emergence of new and improved cryptocurrencies widely known as anonymous cryptocurrencies. Dash is categorized as an anonymous cryptocurrency. Also known as digital cash, Dash is a viable altcoin. It was formerly referred to as Xcoin and then Darkcoin before receiving the name "Dash." The Dash platform conducts transactional procedures through an open-source, peer-to-peer mechanism, as seen in the Bitcoin platform. Additionally, the platform uses PrivateSend (private transactions), InstaSend (instant transactions) and DGBB (decentralized governance). The Dash cryptocurrency became the first decentralized autonomous organization through its budgeting systems and the introduction of DGBB.

Its inventors' vision is to create virtual cash which can be used to conduct online transactions in different countries. In other words, it was created to act as a national online currency.

THE ANNALS OF DASH

On the 18th of January 2014, Evan Duffield, Dash's developer, introduced the cryptocurrency (then known as Xcoin) to the Internet. Its name was subsequently changed to Darkcoin and then, in March 2015, Evan introduced the current name, Dash (a blend of "digital" and "cash"). He said that after looking into the phenomenal mechanism of Bitcoin, he realized that Bitcoin transactions were not as fast as they could be. He knew he could improve on that but no Bitcoin developer would create room for such alterations, as it would require changing some basic codes on its network. Hence, he created the Dash cryptocurrency.

One million, nine hundred thousand million Dash coins, about a quarter of the current amount in circulation, were mined just two days after the introduction of Dash. The influx of the mined coins within those two days was referred to as "instamine." Later, Duffield said that the instamine was an incorrect calculation due to an error code which used a corrupt value to calculate subsidy. After the glitch was fixed, stakeholders rejected his suggestion of a re-launch without the inclusion of "instamine." Also, Evan's idea to spread the initial production through what he termed an "airdrop" didn't sit well with investors, who turned down this idea as well. Duffield gave up on the reform and allowed the platform to continue with its growth.

Dash is one of the very few cryptocurrencies that survived the array of scams which dominated the Internet around the time of its 2014 launch. Currently, the Dash Core Team, comprised essentially of the Dash community developers, includes about 50 employees. While about 30 of them are full-time developers, others work on a part-time basis. The team also consists of volunteers whom the administrators do not directly pay. The core developers do not rely on donations or contributions that could create conflicts within the system. Rather, they are paid from the platform's budget. Dash continues to thrive because of its successful solutions to confirmation times, decentralized governance and block sized increments.

MARKET CAPITALIZATION

Dash's trade volume is about $100 million a day, which makes the sum of its market cap around $1.5 billion. A dash is valued at around $240, making it among the 10 most valuable cryptocurrencies currently in circulation. The Dash community is constantly expanding. On the BitcoinTalk website, more than 6,400 pages are devoted to Dash, making it the site's most active cryptocurrency platform. It has about eight million reads and 153,000 replies.

DASH COIN SUPPLY

It is expected that a total of 18 million coins will be mined and supplied on Dash. Currently, about 7.5 million dash coins are in circulation. According to that calculation, the total supply of dash will be used up in the year 2300. Like Ethereum, the Dash blockchain has a mining time of about two-and-a-half minutes, which is four times as fast as the Bitcoin blockchain. However, Dash has a 7.1 percent yearly decrease in its block rewards.

MINERS AND MASTERNODES

Dash's platform is powered by a two-level administrative structure. The first structure or division consists of the miners who program and process transactions on the blockchain. They are equally responsible for the security of all transactions within the platform.

The second division houses the masternodes, who are entitled to higher nodes. The nodes are responsible for processing the PrivateSend and InstaSend features. Such functions earn the masternodes a 45 percent block reward. They also have access to special features like the governance function within the Dash cryptocurrency network. Essentially, possessing 1,000 dash coins gives users the ability to join the masternodes.

Although 1,000 dash coins can be used at any point in time, this simply dissociates such masternodes from the network. It was introduced as a form of wager against any Sybil attack. Due to their important functions, the masternodes receive rewards equal to the miners. After the distribution of 90 percent of new block rewards, the budget section claims the remaining 10 percent.

A writer, editor and developer, Eric Sammons, who has a passion for cryptocurrencies and technological economics in general, said that Dash's biggest strength is its masternode program. He suggested that the second-level network is the main reason for Dash's ability to integrate innovative programs which Bitcoin still cannot afford to integrate. Some of these programs include the Dash budget system, private send and instant send. Although he was no different from many others who fell in love with Bitcoin at the onset, he was smitten by the intelligence applied in its build.

Sammons noted, however, that when the Bitcoin platform descended into an unsettled network with no visible solution, he began looking into other cryptocurrencies. He realized that while other digital currencies offered advantages over Bitcoin, Dash's masternode network tackled the principal issues affecting Bitcoin's efficiency and thus provided perfect solutions for them.

He said that Dash neutralized the recurring doublespending issues with Bitcoin, reduced the time required to validate transactions and addressed the unavailability of a governance structure.

FUNDING AND MANAGEMENT

Sammons said that in contrast to other digital currencies' teams of developers, Dash's developers seek only to develop the platform, not to participate in arguments on Reddit, create censors for competitors or mock those who contribute to other platforms. Sammons said that from his position, those differences matter because a successful digital currency in the payments sector must have a team of qualified professionals as its developers and facilitators.

As mentioned earlier, Dash is the first malware-proof

decentralized autonomous organization whose funding procedures and governance are largely decentralized. Developmental funding and network changes are constantly discussed in the platform's "budget" section. This section, generally characterized by the DGBB ideology, is an avenue for reaching agreement on suggestion for the platform's development. The 10 percent of earnings that goes to the section is used to finance projects that improve the network's functionality. Also, part of the reward is used to employ developers, fund conferences, foster Dash's integration with major exchange sites and engage the services of other active contributors.

Cheah, a cryptocurrency enthusiast on Steemit, said she believed that Dash's adoption by many merchant sites was important to the platform's future and growth. Cheah said there was no reason to own digital money that could not be spent. She said it could be used for remittance payments but Dash cannot yet be obtained in many countries. Cheah said that currently the rush for Dash exists mostly in Europe and North America because those are the regions where available merchants can be found. This also means that Dash may face a surplus.

Furthermore, masternodes constantly suggest development projects, although not all suggestions are funded. Usually, every masternode participant has one vote in the selection process. Those suggestions with many votes become viable. On occasions when the available funds cannot cover the total number of suggestions, only those suggestions with the highest number of votes are processed for implementation. Before the voting stage, discussions are usually held on Dash-related websites such as DashCentral and general Dash forums. Those who have suggested projects receive room to provide details about their suggestions and to convince Dash investors to enlist their projects for voting. Once a project has received sufficient votes, the funds are released automatically through a monthly generated super block. In September 2015, the budget section released $14,000, which has increased since then. Due to the community's growth, the budget section releases as much as $650,000 monthly for suggested projects. On the platform, these projects' positive impacts influence the value of Dash. This ultimately boosts the funds that the section provides.

THE DASH TECHNOLOGY

PRIVATESEND: Formerly known as DarkSend, PrivateSend is a CoinJoin-based inclusion on the Dash network which is essentially used in mixing coins. The process of mixing ensures that all coins have equal value. It offers an array of features which include the adoption of master nodes in place of a website, where mixed masternodes are used for chaining and the approving of mixed coins for only a set of Dash's denominations. One thousand dash is the highest amount of dash that can be used for PrivateSend transactions. In addition, masternodes use PrivateSend to input transactions with the help of a network called DSTX. This process boosts users' privacy by compiling and combing identical inputs from different users into one transaction. The compilation makes the tracing of transactions extremely difficult. The movement of funds within the system also becomes less clear. For instance, Dash allows users to transfer funds privately by including the transfer with multiple transactions. This makes it hard for anyone to differentiate between transactions.

INSTANTSEND: Formerly known as InstantX, InstantSend allows users to process Dash transactions almost instantly. Although the fees involved in using the service for transactions are higher than normal transaction fees, users can transact within one and a half seconds. Usually, transactions are validated through an agreement in the masternodes system. If an agreement is not made at a specific point, the verification process is achieved through standard block procedures. In addition, the InstantSend service helps find solutions to double-spending situations.

DASH'S ACQUISITION OPTIONS

The Dash cryptocurrency can be easily purchased from the Changelly website. Instant exchanges from other cryptocurrencies to Dash are also available on the site, as it currently supports about 55 cryptocurrencies. Essentially, the buyer must provide their Dash address–that is, the specific location where the dash would be stored.

Shapeshift is another website where exchanges from other supported cryptocurrencies to Dash are allowed.

DASH WALLETS

It is generally not advisable to store cryptocurrencies on exchange sites for long periods of time. A few days is ideal but users must secure their coins as soon as they can.

Dash's official website offers basic knowledge for those who are interested. Its principal wallet is built on Bitcoin's QT wallet. However, it has some custom modifications that any user conversant with it would be able to manipulate within a short period of time. Dash's well-known programs, like InstantX and Darksend, have been integrated into the network. Through Darksend, payments can be made anonymously from any part of the world. On the other hand, InstantX is employed in sending an instant transaction which uses the masternode system for verification before miners can add it to a block.

Some of these wallets are:

Dash Mobile Wallets: This is for those who prefer the use of smartphones.

Dash Desktop Wallets: This is the official Dash core wallet which has a standard structured wallet and P2P Client. InstantSend, PrivateSend, Governance and masternode management features are also included in Dash desktop wallets.

Dash Paper Wallet: With support for storing private and public Dash keys, the Dash paper wallet is another secure place in which to store Dash. It is arguably the cheapest medium as well.

THE FUTURE OF THE DASH CRYPTOCURRENCY

The latter months of 2017 will witness the introduction of "Dash Evolution," which promises to expand Dash's accessibility and usability, spreading its popularity to a larger population in the process. Thus, its value is bound to increase. On its website, top 10 reviews provided thoughtful insight. It captions read that long ago, a developer with the Dash platform had plans to include "IP obfuscation" to make transactions more anonymous. Likewise, additional features such as automatic payment processing have not yet been implemented. Retailer acceptance has also been low. However, for as much as three dollars per Dash coin, the value can be said to be relatively high since it is an altcoin. In addition, Dash is unique because it continues to increase in value, doubling its capitalization. More importantly, while the digital currency era is still fairly new and plagued with uncertainties, Dash has achieved a dominant status in the sector. Therefore, if participants are particular about transacting anonymously from different parts of the world, or are seeking positive investment prospects, Dash's platform provides value for one's money and helps users make the best decisions.

In addition, from 0.02 dollars in 2014, Dash's value increased by about one million percent. In December 2016, a further increment of about 1,500 percent occurred, significantly increasing its unit price, which was initially $11. Similar cryptocurrencies such as Monero already exist but Dash continues to prove unbeatable due to its accessibility, flexibility and comprehensive structure. It has shown its formidability and its prospects continue to grow. Heavy presence in online platforms such as Dash Reddit, the Dash YouTube channel, the Dash blog, the Dash forum and the Dash Foundation, among others, makes the cryptocurrency relevant and promising.

CoinGecko, a reputable cryptocoin website, conducted an intriguing interview with the inventor of Dash. The next paragraphs explore this interview. CoinGecko's agent asked how long Evan Duffield had been coding and what got him into cryptocurrency.

Duffield said he started coding when he was 15 years old and he was then almost 34 years old. He said he became interested in coding because he felt that it was interesting and then he got more serious in his high school days, when he found some jobs in it. After that he began moving around the corporate sector.

Duffield mentioned that he learned about cryptocurrency in early 2010, although he disregarded the topic for several months. Once he encountered it once more, he decided to check it out. He digested the content of its white paper, after which he conducted some research. He was amazed.

Duffield said that during his younger years, the belief was that cryptocurrencies wouldn't last. However, he realized that blockchain technology, which backs cryptocurrencies, was indeed revolutionary and barrier-breaking. He subsequently discovered that it was a program he needed to explore. He invested some money into it and the investment ultimately yielded good returns, which he found amusing.

CoinGecko's correspondent asked, "How did you get the idea to develop Dash?

Duffield said that in late 2013, he began following Andreas Antonopoulos as well as "Let's Talk Bitcoin." He said he constantly listened to experts' discussions about Bitcoin when the Bitcoin did not have any particular issue in its platform. Duffield noticed that the experts continued to explore how money was related to the network's processes and the state of Bitcoin's fungibility. He said that only such issues were discussed, with no serious attention paid the development's growth. This is unlike the present day, when all talk is centered on development.

Duffield added that such discussions have reached an all-time high as compared to the old talk, which focused attention on the downsides of an absolutely decentralized network whose existence is essentially on the Internet. At the time, there were questions about how the network would grow, how a stable environment would be created without losing the system's fungibility and users' coins, and how users would be informed about privacy infringement and related situations.

He said that he continued to watch and wait for Bitcoin administrators and developers to fix the fungibility problem but nothing was ever done. Then he began to play around with Bitcoin's core client, after which he concluded that he would launch his own digital currency. Duffield said he continued thinking about how to develop a program within the main protocol to correct the persisting problems. He built X11 in a weekend, assembled the program, released it and returned to his regular job on Monday. Duffield said that soon after, he became obsessed with what he had created. This prompted him to resign from his job so that he could fully concentrate on his altcoin.

The agent asked Duffield to explain how Dash's platform makes transactions anonymous. Duffield said that in the Bitcoin network, all transactions can be traced back to coinbase transactions, which are the point of origin of all the coins in the network. Duffield said this point is when the miner or miners originally mined the coins. From there, they moved through the network, from one user to the next.

Duffield said that a careful programmer can follow the procession, and should that programmer find a user's address at a particular point, all the user's activities could be traced. Furthermore, if the programmer identified other addresses after that, the implication was that a transaction had been conducted with another user as well. Duffield said that the proximity between the two addresses increased the chances that a transaction had occurred. He said that in the long run, many of these addresses would be discovered and organizations would begin selling the data. This would indicate a breach in users' privacy; in such a case no one would trust a network prone to such loopholes, including the fact that it is a universal ledger on the network.

Duffield said that Bitcoin developers are aware of the site's shortcomings and have sought a solution through different means. Some of those solutions are centralized servers, requiring that users maintain absolute trust that operators will not seek to obtain their money. Other solutions, while trustworthy, do not guarantee anonymity. Programmers can actually de-anonymize the transaction process without expending too much energy. Duffield said that Bitcoin developers have not found a true way out, although users continue to believe that their activities are completely private and safe, when in the actual sense, they are not.

Duffield then mentioned this lingering problem is what his altcoin (Dash) wants to address. He wanted a network in which users would not necessarily have to trust the party on the other end of the transaction. He believes that such conditions would eliminate concerns that "bad guys" would cart away users' coins or discover their true identities. Furthermore, Duffield said he wanted the platform to be accessible to every user and foster general positive feedback from every stakeholder.

Evan said he built his cryptocurrency to include programs which provide certain services that help users transfer their coins in a trustworthy manner. On Dash, a user merges with other users, and everyone tenders denominated coins. For example, every participant exposes their wallet in a situation in which everyone has coins in increments of 10 and 50. The money is put forward and mixed up. Then arises the question of how much each participant has surrendered. The ultimate implication is that even though the participants are aware of the number of coins they had put forward, no one would be able to differentiate their bills, making the coins anonymously owned. Duffield said this explanation describes the platform's structure.

CoinGecko's agent asked about the meanings and functions of masternodes and InstantX. Duffield said that masternodes are special servers within the platform which provide basic services like mixing procedures. He said these programs can be accessed at any point in time and prompted to execute services like syncing the user's client. He added that Darksend is one of the services they offer, while others include the provision of instant transactions through InstantX.

He said that the process through which InstantX features are provided in the system is straightforward. One could imagine a scenario in which a transaction is publicized within a platform that uses the peer-to-peer pattern; the nearest peers determine the authenticity of such transactions. However, Duffield mentioned that users would not be able to ascertain whether the entire system would accept that.

He then said, *"Dash solves this by sending a transaction to the network and as it propagates across the network, there's a few predetermined masternodes for that given transaction that are selected. These act as a decentralized oracle for the system. They are the ones who tell the network whether the transaction is accepted or not. If you can get a majority of masternodes to say that they accept the transaction then the transaction will be accepted by the miners."*

Duffield also said that other things that seemed to conflict with those that had been accepted would be declined, meaning that the input would be locked, thereby making it unavailable to spend during other transactions. According to Duffield, this technique would eliminate the problem of doublespending. Consequently, users would be able to transact instantly during physical meetings. Users could then depart safely as soon as the transaction was successfully processed.

More questions came from CoinGecko's representative. He asked Duffield to explain the idea and purpose of the Dash Foundation.

Duffield said that when the foundation was created, he used Linux and Bitcoin's foundation. Subsequently, he decided that the foundation's main vision involved setting up a form of decentralized administrative structure in the network's domain. He said that the Dash Foundation's specific function at that time was to offer advice to the main team as well as the altcoin itself. Their duty wasn't to pay their developers' salaries. Foundation members would also not make any decisions about how money would be spent within the platform. Duffield repeated that members do not have to involve themselves in situations other than giving advice to him and other prominent developers in the network.

He said, *"What we have set up is a governance system which uses the masternode network as something like a decentralized senate. There is a limitation on how many can actually exist so we can query these masternodes and their operators on how they feel about given situations in the network. They can actually decide on that within the currency which mean[s] the core team doesn't decide anything. We query the network itself and the network tells us what the preferred course of action is. For example, if we are talking about raising the block limit and half of the community wanted it and the other half didn't. What would happen is we would have public debates between community members, core members, and we would try to educate the public. Then after that period of time has elapsed, we would query the masternode network to decide which direction to go. It solves things efficiently, quickly and is completely tamper-proof."*

CoinGecko's agent asked whether Dash worked alongside Bitcoin or if Bitcoin was a competitor.

Duffield said that Dash was definitely a competitor to Bitcoin. He said that with Bitcoin, Nakamoto found the Proof-of-Work algorithm, and he and other developers stopped working on the main protocol. Duffield said it was then that all the innovations occurred on the platform's edges. With Dash, he tested the core. He soon discovered a significant opportunity for creativity. The masternode program, the incentive programs, the constantly used economics, InstantX and Darksend were all implemented one after the other into Dash's core, creating a much more decentralized system with added value. Duffield said the additions made his digital currency a better option and that his goal was to achieve an absolutely decentralized economy.

Duffield said that, as an example, Bitcoin depends on organizations such as Coinbase to provide the programs that investors or participants use for conversion within the platform. Once a section of the Dash network's important components has been tweaked, a similar feature can be introduced. Only then would it be decentralized.

He also said that Dash would have an economy distinct from that of Bitcoin. In addition, their architectures would not follow the same pattern. Dash's network would ultimately become more resourceful than Bitcoin's network, eventually having an edge through the provision of limitless decentralization.

The correspondent asked if Duffield could establish that he was striving for Dash to become a digital form of cash.

Duffield said that he and the core developers had begun plans to make Dash a digital form of cash. They were seeking a robust solution to provide all the attributes of cash in a currency such as Bitcoin. He said that at the time, Dash was 100 percent fungible and worked almost like normal cash. However, a persisting problem was that it was still too complex for an average individual to manipulate. He couldn't equate Dash to cash at that point in time because, in his opinion, it was too complex to operate. However, he said that addressing this complexity was his next assignment.

FINAL THOUGHTS

Sammons said he had been in the cryptocurrency sector for many years, switching from Bitcoin to other cryptocurrencies. He said that what Satoshi had created could change the world. However, Bitcoin might not be the propellant or catalyst. He believes in competitions among cryptocurrencies and hopes such competition will yield a worldwide currency that is reliable and decentralized.

He believes Dash is in a perfect position to win such competitions. This is not because Dash is complete in every sense, but that its architecture may enable it to cope with developments and blend into future enhancement projects. This means that the strengths of Dash overshadow its weaknesses.

CHAPTER 5: ZCASH (ZEC)

Pieter Gorsira, a developer and founder in the blockchain and cryptocurrency space, said the era of privacy and anonymous coins in cryptocurrencies is here and gaining ground. When these new forms of cryptocurrencies are examined from a technical point of view, the leading cryptocurrency would arguably be Zcash. Notable institutions are participating in the network, and the platform has been adequately integrated into the cryptocurrency community. Gorsira said that different sectors have expressed interest in Zcash, with an increased rate of hashing power since its launch.

Just as with other features in this category, only time will determine the winners and losers. Even the team behind Zcash has continuously discussed how their innovation can be effectively integrated into other networks, such as the Ethereum blockchain.

Gorsira also said that when this occurs, will there be any advantage for Zcash? By the time that happens, the cryptocurrency may have gained such ground among anonymous platforms that its sidelining would be practically impossible. What will happen in years to come may be intriguing.

Zcash is an open-source cryptocurrency which thrives on peer-to-peer cryptographic research. Apart from its decentralized activities, Zcash provides privacy and optional transparency of transactions. In a nutshell, Zcash's outstanding feature as compared to Bitcoin is a high level of privacy.

In an interview conducted on the 20th of January 2016, Zcash's inventor, Zooko Wilcox, shared some ideas forming the basis of his invention. He said that privacy is important when one is trying to uphold specific virtues such as morality, dignity and intimacy. Furthermore, he said that privacy must be consensual. Everyone should be able to decide which actions, movements and words they want to make public. He said that individuals have the right to record their lives with or without the awareness of their employers, family members, neighbors and acquaintances. Wilcox said that if anyone is told that they no longer have the right to privacy in the modern world, they should reject such an assertion. Zcash believes that privacy is crucial in certain commercial situations. Organizations require privacy to run many of their transactions; with a doubt, it cuts across different types of companies.

Wilcox also said he was surprised when he started talking to businesses about Zcash and received positive responses from the financial technology sector. He said they had been developing "blockchain technology" programs, and they had suddenly discovered that they were moving towards a closed road because their customers–that is, banks–had concluded the whole time that Zcash's blockchain technology program came with some sort of privacy, which was not correct. Wilcox also said that financial institutions as well as their customers require privacy in their financial transactions. He said that privacy is very important for commercial situations. Furthermore, Wilcox said that a currency, due to its fungible nature, requires privacy so that it remains a viable medium of exchange in the long run. He added that fungibility is the property which assumes that every coin has been created to be equal. For example, when an individual agrees to give someone $20 and the individual has two $20 bills, whichever bill the other person receives does not matter because the two bills have the same value. Their previous owners also do not have any influence over the bills' worth. Wilcox said that such transactions are necessary for large volumes of commercial activity.

In addition, he said, *"If, every time someone were going to accept money, they had to think about the consequences of accepting this particular payment vs. some other payment of the same amount, commerce would grind to a halt, or would be limited to small groups of shared trust. In an open and programmable financial system, financial privacy is the only way to ensure fungibility."*

Wilcox also said that he knew privacy was a social value. He believes that privacy enhances social ties as well as social institutions. It protects communities and ensures peace and prosperity.

He said that privacy is popular among wealthy communities, and that a lack of privacy is usually seen in poor and underdeveloped communities. As everyone moves their lives to the Internet, integrating their lives with those of others from different parts of the world, Zcash's developers hope to create a brand-new community in which users can prosper and be at peace.

Zcash's developers used Bitcoin's core codes to structure their network. In addition, the "zero-knowledge proof," which is very much an advanced cryptographic technique, is activated in the system to ensure that transactions are verified without detailed information about the process. This means that although Zcash's public blockchain reveals information about payments made within the system, as well as the amount of the transactions, the receivers of the funds and the identities of users who have transferred the funds are kept private.

Hunter Johnson, an associate professor at John Jay College of Criminal Justice, came up with a scenario he felt could occur in the not-too-distant future. He said that if the United States put pressure on Putin through an attack on his staunch supporters' assets and moved to freeze some of the oligarch's banking assets, but if the intended victims knew about these plans before they were initiated, they could convert many of their assets into Bitcoin. Due to the currency's current state of liquidity, such individuals could maintain the living standards they enjoyed before the conversion. They could finance every aspect of their lives with the coins, as many sites accept it as a medium of payment for goods and services. However, the addresses attached to those bitcoins could be traced. The United States government could then decide to ban all platforms from accepting payments from those addresses, automatically ending the coins' life and value.

Wilcox presented some questions: *"What will happen then? Will exchanges cooperate? Will Bitcoin crash? Will the effort be irrelevant as the target continues to use Russian exchanges unhindered? What if the coins get mixed in a coin mixing scheme?"*

He said that if those Putin supporters had converted their assets and savings to ZEC, no government would be able to tamper with their transactions because senders are usually hidden within the platform. Even exchange platforms would not be able to activate a ban.

Wilcox also said that when Zcash was introduced, the development team focused its attention on the platform's stability and security. They also ensured the constant production of software packages as well as supported external programmers who sought to produce innovative programs such as exchanges and wallets for the platform.

THE ANNALS OF ZCASH

Zcash, formerly referred to as Zerocash, experienced a revolution in 2014 when a group of cryptographers from the Institute of Technology and Tel Aviv University decided to work together with Zerocoin developers at Johns Hopkins University in Baltimore, USA. The programmers created a private and efficient cryptocurrency platform by inputting major adjustments to Zerocash.

In January 2016, Zooko Wilcox-O'Hearn, the CEO of ZECC, officially publicized Zcash. It was tagged as the evolution of the already existing Zerocoin cryptocurrency, which originated in the computer department at Johns Hopkins University. Through a new cryptographic procedure, Zcash users can transact within the network without exposing their identities or transaction figures. Zcash became a fully distinct cryptocurrency, breaking free from its attachment to Bitcoin.

The 1.0.0 "sprout" was the first-ever-mined Zcash (zec). It was created on October 28, 2016. By April 2017, Zcash had attained a level of popularity in the digital currency world, earning the platform a pass on the "jaxx" e-wallet. Also during that period, Zcash rose to a high-ranking position among other valuable cryptocurrencies.

CORE COMPONENTS

zk-SNARKs

The acronym zk-SNARK represents "Zero-Knowledge Succinct Non-Interactive Argument of Knowledge." Zk-SNARK is a type of zero-knowledge cryptography introduced in Zcash. Essentially, zk-SNARK proofs provide the high level of privacy found in the Zcash network. This is why Zcash-protected transactions can be successfully encrypted within its blockchain and still be validated. Zk-SNARK also allows users to claim ownership of some pieces of information without any hindrance from third parties and without having to reveal the content of such information.

The zero-knowledge feature lets a user determine that a particular set of information is genuine simply because the user has claimed the information to be true. In other words, the claimer is not obliged to provide further proof to the other user. This way, transactions do not require explicit details and the "proof of knowledge" procedures in Zcash expressly corroborate its developers' vision. Details about how Zcash employs the zk-SNARK mechanism are discussed below.

Christian Lundkvist, a blockchain nerd, ethereal explorer and mystic mathematician, interpreted zk-SNARK's function as follows:

"Suppose Bob is given a hash H of some value, and he wishes to have a proof that Alice knows the value s that hashes to H. Normally Alice would prove this by giving S to Bob, after which Bob would compute the hash and check that it equals H. However, suppose Alice doesn't want to reveal the value s to Bob but instead she just wants to prove that she knows the value. She can use a zk-SNARK for this."

In addition, a response is necessary if a transaction is valid or otherwise to ensure that zero-knowledge privacy has occurred. The program that verifies transactions must ensure that this process occurs within the system, leaving the calculations unknown. This procedure in Zcash is conducted by infusing the cryptocurrency's generally accepted codes into zk-SNARKs. Zk-SNARKs, on the other hand, changes what users are about to prove to some equations, which are then assessed by users in charge of validation, with no form of information leak.

Also, Zcash permits transparent transactions. These sorts of transactions are completely insecure. This happens when a protected address lacks key units and the hardware to create a protected transaction. Thus, transparent addresses can transfer information to protected addresses while transferring the same information to another transparent location. Another loophole is the possibility of falsely obtaining IP addresses to conduct transactions. However, Zcash allows for the use of I2P, Tor and some VPNs to protect IP addresses.

HOW ZK-SNARKS ARE APPLIED TO CREATE A SHIELDED TRANSACTION

Input and output values and the sender's and receiver's addresses are all linked and published on Bitcoin's public blockchain to verify transactions. Zcash, on the other hand, conceals important information, addresses and transaction amounts while still ensuring that transactions are validated within the system. This is done using zk-SNARKs. In Zcash, the user who has sent a transaction comes up with the proof that the input values are equal to the output values of every transfer. The user also ascertains that he/she has permission to spend with the possession of private keys. Because the sender's private keys are cryptographically connected to a signature within the entire transaction, a third part cannot tamper with such transactions.

Other publicly generated keys are distributed within Zcash's network to its users. These keys are widely regarded as verifying keys, and they are essentially used to create and examine proofs during transactions. A sender uses the keys to generate a proof that the information the sender has provided is valid. Afterwards, miners ascertain that the sender has observed all the rules within the system with their verifying keys. About 40 seconds are required to send and process transactions in Zcash, while the validation occurs within milliseconds. This implies that the sender always has more inputs than the receiver.

Blocking the links between transactions is a common method other cryptocurrencies use to create privacy for users. However, the possibility of storing encrypted Zcash transactions on the blockchain has created new developments in the cryptocurrency world. This means users still get privacy even though their transactions are published on public blockchains. Developers believe that later versions of the Zcash network will give users room to select, using their intuition, the transactions they would or would not like to protect.

The Zcash support team said that it is currently trying to ensure that protected addresses become easier to use. For instance, some developmental plans for Zcash range from payment offloading to payment disclosure. These features would usher in many positive offers for third-party participants.

MINING ZCASH

The Equihash algorithms used to mine Zcash make it resistant to the Application-Specific Integrated Circuit (ASIC). Also, GPUs and CPUs are interchangeably used in mining Zcash coins.

FUTURE APPLICATIONS OF ZK-SNARKS

Apart from generating protected and secure transactions in Zcash, there are other probable applications for zk-SNARKs. Although its developers are still perfecting another clear-cut function, Zk-SNARKs can already be used to validate relations without exposing vital information.

At present, a zero-knowledge security level could be used in any community's ledger through Zcash's method of applying zk-SNARKs. Since zk-SNARK developers are also the core research on the Zcash platform, constant developmental tasks are in progress to ensure that zk-SNARK's usability soon expands beyond the Zcash community.

CHAPTER 6: THE GRIDCOIN (GRC)

Gridcoin is an open-source cryptocurrency which rewards research based on BOINC projects. It shares some similarities with Bitcoin, which is proof of the stake scheme. These BOINC projects could range from finding cures for epidemic diseases to seeking solutions for inexplicable events. Although a fixed amount of coins is given out in the platform daily, the situation is different from Bitcoin's protocol in the sense that miners must compete to earn Gridcoins.

Halford, Gridcoin's developer, said in an exclusive interview with Crypt.la that he saw how Bitcoin's price rose from one cent to $500 dollars per bitcoin, and he found it hard to understand the volume of heat that got consumed in general. He said that one day he began thinking about ways in which clock cycles could be used for more productive tasks than searching for solved suffixes. He began developing plans to make BOINC tasks for proof-of-work schemes. Ultimately, Halford came up with a new cryptocurrency.

In addition to its proof-of-stake algorithm, the research rate of users is equally rewarded based on the importance of their research. Through a platform named Neural Network, stakeholders usually reach an agreement about the quality and quantity of research carried out on some BOINC projects that must have been listed at an earlier time on the platform.

The decision determines the number of coins the research earns.

The Gridcoin research team said that Gridcoin gives out rewards for carrying out genuine tasks. The platform's goal is to convert some measures of computing powers expended on hashes that are relatively wasteful to resourceful ones. This would lead to the creation of supercomputing clusters that accept different forms of research and advancement in technology. Large organizations and colleges covet supercomputers' accessibility. However, the creation of a huge network of computers, which was once unachievable, is no longer impossible. The BOINC is a very open community that accepts every type of change in technology and hardware. The program provided supercomputing processes for more than a decade. It was restricted to users who could donate their resources willingly.

THE ANNALS OF GRIDCOIN

Gridcoin was launched on the 16th of October 2013. It is equally accessible to anyone around the world. Its developer is Rob Halford, although this name is a pseudonym. In 2014 there was a transition from "Gridcoin Classic" (the original version of Gridcoin) to "Gridcoin Research." Before the transition, Gridcoin Classic used a combination of proof-of-work and proof-of-stake algorithms. Soon after, it was discovered that a huge amount of resources was being wasted through the hybrid mechanism that Gridcoin Classic employed. Hence, a need existed to change from scrypt mining to the proof-of-research and proof-of-stake algorithms.

FEATURES

Gridcoin or GRC is a decentralized network whose transactions are conducted cryptographically through a peer-to-peer system. This way, there is absolutely no need for third parties in transactions. In total, there are about four million users who have registered with Gridcoin, while 500,000 stakeholders are active within the platform. This means that Gridcoin's platform already has considerable computing power for research.

Steven Gleiser, an analyst at Bitcoin Chaser, said it is principally a program that permits users to willingly put forward their computing resources for use by other important programs that need them. The program is an open source one that uses a system which can duplicate the measure of computing power available for projects. Hence, for those who buy into the values of conducting research and an economy with lower carbon, and who have computer power they can volunteer to provide solutions to important problems, Gridcoin is the platform to join.

Because Gridcoin is an open source platform, users from different parts of the world can take part in all transactions simultaneously. In addition, Gridcoin transaction fees are very low compared to those of other platforms.

Other features include its decentralized voting system that lets users participate freely and stay informed.

In a brief post, the founder of Razor's Forex Trading Blog, Traderman, said that apart from Gridcoin's ability to transfer a good amount of financial incentives to participants in every part of the world, thereby contributing to scientific advancements, it also has the potential to carry out commercial tasks such as financial data modelling and renditions in 3D. Even with these, numerous other programs would fit comfortably into the platform. Based on an analysis on the BOINC website, about 900,000 computers are participating in its projects and there are about 200,000 volunteers. These figures seem to be impressive but when compared to the number of computers in the world, it is a minute figure.

EARNING GRIDCOIN AS A REWARD FOR BOINC COMPUTATIONS

With the DPOR reward process, approximately 50,000 Gridcoins are created daily. The following are ways to earn Gridcoins after computations.

SOLO CRUNCHING: Through continuous stakes, users help broadcast transactions and secure the currency's network. This process is monitored across many BOINC and Gridcoin websites. In return for constant stakes, users earn coins.

POOL CRUNCHING: With pool crunching, users do not need previously purchased Gridcoins before they earn additional units. Gridcoins are earned at a faster rate through pool crunching as compared to solo crunching. This is because of the advantage of higher computational power. However, users can decide to withdraw their contributions from pool crunching and return to solo crunching as soon as they have adequate balances for doing so.

As easy and efficient as solo crunching is, it tends to create room for centralization within the network. Furthermore, fees are charged for earnings in pool crunching.

THE RELEVANCE OF GRIDCOIN

Apart from the successful transactions conducted within its network, Gridcoin is a cryptocurrency that has positively influenced the digital world. Through its BOINC research projects, it has caused cryptocurrencies to have a larger and growing audience around the world. Various news outlets have, at one time or another, published articles about Gridcoin's influence and the ideas surrounding its creation.

The Gridcoin wiki said that through the Proof-of-Research scheme, electrical resources which would have been wasted on hash numbers that regulate the platform are used to add value to humans throughout the world. It also causes Gridcoins to consume less energy. The 90-second time block for transactions encourages easier and quicker purchases from buyers.

CHAPTER 7: THE IOTA CRYPTOCURRENCY

The meaning of IOTA: Think of a deviation from the norm; when it comes to cryptocurrency, IOTA fits such a role perfectly. It has the sole aim of spearheading the turn towards machine-to-machine transactions. It was introduced to the Internet in October 2015.

"Iota is a cryptocurrency that aims to establish itself as the fuel for efficient (M2M) transactions." – Cryptojudgement

IOTA switched from the traditional blockchain on which numerous cryptocurrencies are based to Directed Acyclic Graphs (DAG). This relatively new technology is generally referred to as the "Tangle." In essence, transactions on the IOTA platform can be conducted offline and are completely free of charge.

Upon its introduction, 2,779,530,283,277,761 tokens were produced and shared in the ICO. That figure will remain permanent in the platform. SI units are provided in IOTA to quantify prices. For instance, Bitfinex's IOTA trades are processed in units of one million IOTA, which is usually represented as "Mi."

IOTA also has an enabling environment for the Internet of Things (IoT). Once it becomes more accessible and acceptable to unlimited users, multiple online platforms and across the globe, IOTA will change the face of cryptocurrency. Its (ICO) participants already have a high amount of generated revenues but its growth won't stop there.

Currently, Byteball and IOTA are the two cryptocurrencies that use DAG technology. However, the two can't even compete, as the former still attaches charges to its transactions. Since February 2017, the value of IOTA has continued to increase.

Furthermore, IOTA provides a way out of the recurring shortcomings of blockchain-based cryptocurrencies. Some of these noteworthy developments are:

Transaction costs: As said earlier, IOTA is the first cryptocurrency that uses the "Tangle" in place of the blockchain. Different transactions are compiled in the blockchain before they are validated by miners. However, within the Tangle, a new block is formed for every new transaction. Likewise, the block validates itself without any external interference or assistance. IOTA transactions can be conducted only when users have previously validated two transactions chosen randomly within the network. An easy proof-of-work scheme facilitates this process. Thus, transactions are not absolutely feeless. Rather, the costs of transactions are next to nothing because the proof-of-work process is minimal. This enables devices to proceed with any form of dependence.

Scalability: The continuous adoption of scales increases scalability because two previous transactions are validated by a new one within the system. This means the entire system will remain scalable as multiple users continue processing transactions.

Offline transactions: In the IOTA network, offline transactions are carried out. As soon as a node is back online, the subtangles co-join offline transactions to the actual Tangle. This implies that nodes do not necessarily need to be online during a transaction. With this addition, the functionality of applications in many sections instantly increases.

THE IOTA TOKEN

IOTA mining is not required, as all the IOTA tokens that will ever be in circulation have already been mined and inputted into the network. The 2,779,530,283,277,761 IOTA tokens that were pre-mined have successfully promoted micropayments as well as the use of minimal amounts of value for transactions.

In the last quarter of 2015, IOTA held an ICO. A total of 1.337 BTC was raised during that period. Currently, IOTA are exchanged on a less-secure platform. Nonetheless, the value of IOTA has constantly increased. One million IOTA is valued as 000024 BTC, making the market capitalization of IOTA around 66.708 BTC. In the coin market, IOTA is ranked as the 14th most credible cryptocurrency.

THE IOTA TEAM AND FOUNDATION

Sergey Ivancheglo, Sergei Popov, Dominik Schiener and David Sonstebo are the principal developers who created the IOTA foundation in Germany. With the help of other noted workers, these computer geeks have tailored IOTA's affairs since its inception. The team has continued growing, but there is still room for improvement, perhaps in the area of social media, being active in forums, increasing online activity and selling its vision to a larger population. These approaches are required because IOTA has yet to get an exchange launch. This has caused doubts about when it will eventually be used across exchange platforms.

RUNNING AN IOTA WALLET

IOTA has two basic types of wallets. These wallets can be processed as light or full modes. It is, however, advisable that new users adopt the light wallet mode, as it is based on GUI. The server that has the IOTA IRI creates an instant connection to users' wallets. Bitfinex has connected a network of IOTA light wallet servers to ensure that light wallets connect to the servers without glitches. Hence, load balancing servers can help connect any wallet.

Important Notes

Once tokens are uploaded twice or more from a single address in IOTA, the transaction automatically becomes less secure. Users are expected to use new addresses for all new transfers.

Sticky Sessions

A change in a user's IP address in IOTA will ultimately make the load balancing server redirect the user's server to maintain a stable condition among all the servers. This is one of the features of the Tangle on which IOTA's entire network thrives. Balances and history are usually not displayed in full as soon as a node connects to it from a new or different address. However, the load balancer in IOTA will always direct users' requests to a regular server if the user's IP address remains the same. It is therefore recommended that users remain on a single IP.

Snapshots

Upon the completion of snapshots in IOTA, full and light wallet severs' databases are erased from the network, removing balances and history in the process. However, users can retrieve their balances and transaction history by repeatedly creating addresses.

CHAPTER 8: DIGIBYTE (DGB)

DigiByte is a decentralized digital currency which thrives on the DigiByte blockchain. The blockchain was created in 2013 but not launched until January 2014. As with other altcoins, DigiByte is similar in some ways to Bitcoin, although its blockchain has noticeable improvements and additions. Some of these additions are improved security and a 15-second block time. DigiByte remains the longest publicly shared blockchain in the history of cryptocurrency. It had an amazing $230 million as its market capitalization in June 2017.

Mike Biss said that DigiByte is a blockchain-based technology created to compete and outdo normal financial transactions.

He said the digital currency seeks to *"push the capability limits of this emerging technology, it brings improvements to overall security along with many other benefits for literally everyone. This is a seriously good idea and it hasn't found us a moment too soon, already with three yearsof continuous development and integrity under its belt, it is also a seriously juicy looking investment as it is currently almost certainly outrageously undervalued when compared with many 'apparently' more popular cryptos."*

THE ANNALS OF DIGIBYTE

Jared Tate, DigiByte's developer, created the cryptocurrency to offer a more decentralized network than that found in Bitcoin. Tate also ensured that DigiByte is faster and more secure than Bitcoin. Even though DigiByte was pre-mined to reward its early users and developers, its first block was mined in January 2014. With Digishield, DigiByte became the first cryptocurrency to use difficulty retargets. This feature is now found in many other cryptocurrencies.

FEATURES

Peter Paul, a blogger and trader on a daily and weekly basis, said that DigiByte relates more to Bitcoin than to Dash. He said that it seeks to create a new means of transaction procedures. Its masternodes program, which makes transactions very quick, proves this assertion. Paul maintained that although the process is slow and has size limits, Bitcoin has a standard and reliable structure within its blockchain. DigiByte, on the other hand, is a cryptocurrency that plays on a new field while offering better techniques for mining.

DigiByte's adoption of multi-algorithm mining procedures makes it a pioneer in the field. Before DigiByte, only the proof-of-work algorithm was used across all cryptocurrency networks.

Furthermore, DigiByte implemented Segregated Witness (SegWit), becoming the second mainstream platform to use the program. The inclusion of Segregated Witness in its blockchain created room for the implementation of atomic swaps, chain transactions and lighting networks.

DIGISHIELD

Digishield is a hardfork which ensures that the DigiByte blockchain guards against multi-pools that use low difficulty to mine a huge number of DigiByte's coins. After its successful integration into the platform, Digishield has been used effectively on other platforms, such as Zcash and Dogecoin.

MULTI-ALGO

Multi-algo is a form of hardfork which permits multiple algorithms for mining. The program was launched to enhance and assist GPU and CPU mining, ASIC mining and other proof-of-work schemes simultaneously within the blockchain. DigiByte's integration of different mining schemes allows more miners to participate in the mining process. Therefore, transactions and activities within the network are more decentralized.

MULTI-SHIELD

The multi-shield program was launched in December 2014. It is a hard fork developed to initiate the multi-algo program. The multi-shield was also used to initiate different forms of mining pools within the blockchain.

DIGI-SPEED

The digi-speed program was integrated into DigiByte's network to increase transaction speed in the blockchain. Essentially, transaction speeds timed around 30 seconds were reduced by 50 percent.

TECHNOLOGY

The expectation is that in 2035, 21 billion Digicoins will have been mined. This has been set as the maximum number of coins that will ever be mined on the platform. As of 2017, more than eight billion DigiByte coins are in circulation.

MINING ALGORITHMS

As mentioned earlier, DigiByte uses multiple mining schemes. These schemes include the SHA 256 algorithm, scrypt algorithm, Groestl algorithm, skein algorithm and the Qubit algorithm.

COMMUNITIES

DigiByte currently has six communities for its blockchain and currency. These communities are:

Digihash: The Digihash is a mining pool which supports the scrypt, skein, Qubit and SHA 256 algorithms. Fees acquired from these mining pools are remitted to the developers to help regulate the currency.

Digisign: This is a smart contract-based program which helps users securely conduct and validate transactions and documents in general through a decentralized process. It uses the SHA 256 hash, which means transactions are cryptographically stored on the blockchain.

DigiByte Gaming: This program gives gamers within the network an opportunity to play popular games and earn coins. The coins are earned based on performance in games and competitions.

DigiByte Tip: As found in Dogecoin, the DigiByte tip offers similar services. It lets users gift DigiByte's coins to one another on social media networks such as Twitter and Reddit.

WALLETS

Wallets such as gaming wallets, Jaxx wallets, Coinomi wallets, DigiByte Android, DigiByte Core Mac and DigiByte Core Windows are used to store DigiByte coins and private keys and addresses.

EXCHANGE PLATFORMS

Due to DigiByte's popularity, there are a few notable communities where it can be exchanged and used in transactions. Some of these exchange platforms are Shapeshift, Litebit, Yobit, Cryptopia, Bitrexx and many others.

IMPACT

The decentralized nature of DigiByte's blockchain has attracted many developers who carry out different forms of projects on the blockchain. Already, a play station store accepts Digicoin as a medium for payment. Also, DigiByte Holdings was nominated in 2016 for a Microsoft program, leading to its inclusion on Azure.

DigiByte was also one of the finalists in a technology-based program called Citi Tech for Integrity. In the program, DigiByte was able to present its Digisign program to IBM, Microsoft and Facebook as well as other technology giants.

On its website, FTReporter remarked that DigiByte helps users in 82 nations. Also, the community has taken some steps to increase the number of its participants in other nations that do not yet have access to the platform. Already, a large population is trying to get the best from DigiByte because it remains the only community in which convenience and security are available on a large scale.

CHAPTER 9: DOGECOIN (DOGE)

"I didn't imagine it being anywhere near as popular as it became. I thought it was amusing that people were trading it for things and small amounts of Bitcoin at first. I thought people would mine it because it was silly and maybe months down the line they might trade a million for a Litecoin or something." – Billy Markus

A few weeks after its launch, Dogecoin quickly rose in the ranks of altcoins. The comic origin of its name quickly gave it unprecedented popularity. Doge soon became the fourth most viable cryptocurrency in the world. "Doge" refers to a Shiba Inu dog, which drew attention to the currency. From the date of its launch in December 2013 to January 2014, Dogecoin's market capitalization reached 60 million USD. By June 2017, that number had risen to $340 million.

The creation of a website, a blog, forums and general online awareness quickly gave Dogecoin a relevance on which it still thrives. Activities and developmental programs within its communities also add to the cryptocurrency's rapid development and viability. There has been a yearly increase of 5.256 billion coins since 2015, although 100 billion coins had been in circulation before then. Dogecoins are accepted in a few top-notch commercial outlets and are very popular among users, who give Dogecoins out as a reward for contributing to the platform's development. Little wonder its rise to the mainstream is commonly known as "to the moon."

THE ANNALS OF DOGECOIN

Billy Markus from Portland and an Adobe systems engineer named Jackson Palmer developed Dogecoin. Though Palmer created and registered the domain "dogecoin.com", it was Markus who found the domain fascinating and began some projects to develop it. Soon, he created a wallet for the cryptocurrency. Dogecoin continued to grow and by January 2014 its trade volume had surpassed that of other cryptocurrencies, including Bitcoin. Currently, Dogecoin can be exchanged for goods and services. Also, its forums contain a list of businesses and vendors that accept the currency as a medium of exchange.

THE DOGECHAIN

DogeChain is Dogecoin's database, just as a blockchain is the database for Bitcoin and other cryptocurrencies. However, an important improvement is that DogeChain provides more comprehensive details on transactions and activities that occur within the Dogecoin platform. It has an application programming Interface (API) which explains the way software applications on the network should be maneuvered. DogeChain gives users the ability to access information about the availability of Dogecoins. The API helps users get hassle-free information about a transaction's validity as well as the amounts being transacted. Public key hashes can also be discovered using the API. In addition, DogeChain provides information about the current network power and difficulty levels during mining. It publishes information about block numbers as well as transactions that generally occur within the network

BLOCKS

Dogecoin's block serves as storage for the permanent safekeeping of records. It also functions as a ledger for Dogecoins in a Dogecoin wallet. Each block within the DogeChain is linked to one another–that is, a new block goes beneath the last one.

EXCHANGE PLATFORMS

After the AltQuick exchange platform granted its permission for Dogecoin exchanges, other platforms such as Vault of Satoshi, BTC 38 and Asia Next Gen integrated the Dogecoin exchange into their platforms. A constant amount of 5.2 billion Dogecoins will be produced on a yearly basis. This means the amount of Dogecoins in circulation will ultimately be unlimited. This was confirmed when Palmer publicly said that the mining of Dogecoins would continue and would not end on a certain date. After the initial production of 100 billion coins before 2015, 50 billion have been mined.

TRANSACTIONS

According to CoinMarketCap, transactions within the Dogecoin platform surpass transactions in other cryptocurrency platforms. That rate shows that Dogecoin's main goal is for the currency to be used during transactions and not for storage. Dogecoin transactions are processed using cryptographic keys. While one of the two keys is private, the other is public. The private key easily reads information about the public key. This helps private key holders transact without worrying about the possibility of exposing encrypted information. Dogecoin's public key consists of 34 numbers and letters starting with the letter D. Furthermore, the public key is necessary to use Dogecoins from other users.

On the other hand, a private key creates room for users to access their wallets. It is a password that users must provide to check their account balances.

MINING

Because Dogecoin is a decentralized platform, everyone within the network communicates with each other simultaneously. All transactions within the network are openly confirmed after a certain number of blocks.

Also, Dogecoin miners are required to monitor activities during transactions and also to confirm all transactions in the network. Once Dogecoin miners discover an incoming transaction, they instantly conduct a complex algorithm computation which is usually matched against the block before the one that is about to be created. As soon as the computation is successful, the old block is sealed off while the incoming block can continue saving transactions.

As in other mining processes, the more computing power a miner has, the higher the chances of solving the difficulty hash. Eventually, the miner who successfully discovers a new block earns several coins. Currently, the number of coins earned in every mining period is 500,000. This reward, however, is not constant. The amount of coins rewarded varies from time to time.

CAMPAIGNS

FUNDRAISING: Throughout its history, Dogecoin has been able to raise funds for various purposes. For example, $40,000 was raised for a Jamaican team and an additional $30,000 was realized after the fundraising program. The donation helped the Jamaican team participate in the Olympics.

The Dogecoin Foundation has spearheaded other charitable events. It has continued to raise considerable amounts of money to finance important projects around the world. Other developmental strategies carried out by the Foundation and other stakeholders include the Dogecoin ATM, which was launched in February 2014 in Vancouver, and the development of web applications such as a weather forecasting app. Such efforts have helped keep Dogecoin relevant and reliable. On

Reddit, users can transfer Dogecoins to one another seamlessly. The Reddit-based transaction is widely known as "Dogetipbot."

TIPPING: Users can be tipped an amount of Dogecoins for promoting the cryptocurrency on social media. In addition, tips are available for developmental suggestions and educational content related to Dogecoin.

VERDICT

Dogecoin's acceptable value and constant accessibility make it a reliable and outstanding digital currency. Although it is impossible to predict its future, currently Dogecoin is a cryptocurrency that shows promise. It has been continuously used as a medium of payment for a wide variety of goods and services.

"We hope that it can become the de facto tipping currency of the internet. Right now it is extremely popular on Reddit and gaining ground on Twitter and Imgur, and we want to spread that to Facebook and Google+ and other social media sites, as well as new media such as TwitchTV and YouTube" – Billy Markus

CHAPTER 10: THE BURSTCOIN (BURST)

In a sector in which the proof-of-stake and the proof-of-work algorithms are dominantly used, Burstcoin is the first digital currency to launch a different algorithm known as the proof-of-capacity algorithm. Although Burstcoin is also based on blockchain technology, its mining process is conducted using the proof-of-capacity algorithm, which makes it different from many other cryptocurrencies. During its mining, miners use ordinary computer storage. This an advantage compared to other expensive methods of mining, such as the one found in Bitcoin. A single coin unit of Burstcoin is referred to as a Burst. Burstcoin is also a Nxt-based digital currency.

A Steemit expert, Lexicon, once said, *"Burst is a green coin meaning it doesn't cost that much electricity to mine and confirm transactions as it uses hard drive space to store hash instead of generating them from a GPU. It is done in a specific way in which the hash is reused, since it is incredibly inefficient to do it via any other method."*

THE ANNALS OF BURSTCOIN

As in many other virtual currencies, a pseudonymous name, "burstcoin," launched the digital currency on BitcoinTalk in August 2014. At its launch, no Burstcoin had been mined yet. That is, Burstcoin is not a pre-mined cryptocurrency. However, the day after it was launched, the Genesis block was created. With it being a project that didn't have any third-party control, users immediately took over the advancement activities within the platform after the original developer, burstcoin, vanished with no explanation. In January 2016, a prominent user of the platform created and launched a forum on BitcoinTalk. Burstcoin's core code is still being developed by experts around the world.

THE VALUE OF BURSTCOIN

The total number of Burstcoins that will ever be mined is 2,158,812,800. An average of 10,000 Burstcoins are mined every four minutes, although the reward for mining is reduced by five percent every month. As mentioned earlier, the cost for mining Burstcoins is considerably low compared to that of other mainstream cryptocurrencies. It uses an Nxt blockchain which creates room for flexibility and advancement. Its decentralized blockchain also creates room for developers to invent personal software or programs within the platform. This is why many consider Burstcoin to be a futuristic cryptocurrency. It is sometimes referred to as 2.0, which is synonymous with an upgrade to other cryptocurrencies such as Bitcoin, which is regarded as cryptocurrency 1.0.

The proof-of-capacity algorithm was first introduced on the Burstcoin platform. Burstcoin is also one of the pioneer cryptocurrencies that launched smart contracts. Innovative activities have been in progress in its smart contracts program, even before smart contracts were launched on Ethereum's network. Furthermore, Burstcoin is the first digital currency to launch automated transactions (ATs) through its smart contracts. AT was the first smart contracts feature successfully run on a blockchain using a decentralized process. Also, cross-chain transactions such as the atomic cross-chain transaction (ACCT) are examples of other innovative programs that Burstcoin pioneered. The ACCT eliminates the need for an online exchange platform during trades. It is a decentralized program which enables the exchange of two different types of cryptocurrencies without third-party involvement.

THE BURSTCOIN BLOCKCHAIN

Being its database, the Burstcoin blockchain stores all transactions that occur within the Burstcoin platform. It is regulated by a string of connected computers known as nodes. These nodes are responsible for running Burstcoin applications. The Burstcoin blockchain is structured in such a way that no central location exists where operations are monitored.

SECURITY

Burstcoin uses private keys that offer the only means for users to transact within the platform. Once a private key is missing or cannot be provided to a user, the Burstcoins in the wallet of that user become useless. For any transaction, a user must provide their private key for verification purposes.

MINING

In the Burstcoin whitepaper, developers such as Stefan Dziembowski, Sebastian Faust, Vladimir Kolmogorov and Krzysztof Pietrzak described how the proof-of-capacity algorithm is used in mining Burstcoins. The first stage of mining Burstcoins is the computation of large data. This data is stored on a computer and is known as plots. As soon as a miner has successfully begun running the plot in the blockchain, a result—referred to as a "deadline"—is used to identify the winner of the block. The miner with the lowest deadline is regarded as the winner of that block. That miner is then given the proceeds from the transaction fees as a reward.

MINING POOLS

Some groups of Burstcoin miners have developed new ways to mine; this is referred to as a mining pool. A mining pool is created because it is generally not easy to quickly identify the smallest deadline within a block. Because mining pools contain combinations of different miners, they provide room for miners to have equally distributed rewards at the end of every block.

FEATURES OF BURSTCOIN

Burstcoin is based on the Nxt platform. This enhances the successful running of many embedded programs. One of its features is the operation of two different types of wallets. The first wallet is an online wallet, while the other is a desktop-based wallet that can be downloaded and installed on computers. This provision lets users access their wallets from different parts of the world. In addition, Android-based wallets are available.

The Burstcoin blockchain also features a program known as the Burst Asset Exchange. It is a platform on which users can trade assets without the interference of third parties. Mining rigs, mining pools and other types of assets are the goods being traded on the Burst Asset Exchange.

Another feature of Burstcoin's blockchain is its smart contracts. The integration of automated transactions in Burstcoin's smart contracts makes transactions seamless, fast and inexpensive. Efficiency is also guaranteed, and smart contracts ensure that all savings within Burstcoin's blockchain are kept secure and stored permanently.

CROWDFUNDING

Burstcoin's network contains a crowdfunding program that allows users to source funds for projects and developmental tasks in a decentralized way.

Furthermore, Burstcoin wallets have an escrow feature which allows third parties to hold a portion of Burstcoins during transactions. This is, of course, done with the consent of the parties involved in the transaction. Within its network, Burstcoin has a market where users can sell goods or items in exchange for other items. These items are usually listed through a display of participants' account IDs.

HOW TRANSACTIONS ARE CONDUCTED IN THE BURSTCOIN NETWORK

Burstcoin transactions are relatively straightforward. The following extract explains the process.

"The sender details the parameters for the required transaction type (sending money, creating an alias, transmitting a message, issuing an asset or an order for an asset). All values for the transaction inputs are bounds checked for validity. If the transaction is found to be valid then the public key for the generating account is computed using the supplied secret passphrase. A new transaction is created, with a type and sub-type value set to match the type of transaction being created. All specified parameters are included in the Transaction object. A unique transaction ID is generated with the creation of the object.

"Subsequently, the transaction is digitally signed using the sending account's private key. Then, the encrypted transaction data is placed within a message instructing network peers to process the transaction. The transaction is ultimately broadcasted to all peers on the network." (Wikipedia)

THE BURST NATION

The Burst Nation is one of the most relevant Burstcoin forums on which issues concerning Burstcoins are constantly discussed.

Personnel from Bitcoinist (an online digital currency discussion platform) talked extensively with a member of the Burst team about BURST and what "decentralized file storage" is actually used for. The discussion went as follows:

The Bitcoinist asked about the differences between Burst and other cryptocurrencies. The Burst team said that BURST can easily be differentiated from other digital currencies. One respondent said that BURST was the world's first proof-of-capacity altcoin. Also, at the time it was the only digital coin with working Turing complete smart contracts in a live surrounding. He also mentioned that the proof-of-capacity algorithm had been fully developed by the principal programmer known by the name "burstcoin" on forums such as BitcoinTalk.

He said that smart contracts ran on a technology referred to as Automated Transactions (AT), which had been developed by CIYAM developers led by Ian Knowles. Furthermore, he said that since BURST was an innovative fork of Nxt, it came with a complete component of other crypto 2.0 programs, including different types of advanced transactions like escrow, assets, messaging and subscription, to name a few. All the programs are straight from BURST's wallet. The respondent maintained that the "unique amalgam" of available technological programs makes BURST different from other digital currencies.

The Bitcoinist agent then asked if the Burst team could describe the proof of capacity (POC).

A respondent said, *"Proof of Capacity is an innovative algorithm that uses storage space to mine. In a nutshell, miners pre-generate chunks of data known as 'plots' which are saved to disk. The size of plot miners storage is effectively what is commonly referred to as hashrate, i.e. your mining 'speed'. The miner will skim every block through the saved plots and come up with an amount of time until it is able to mine a block if another block hasn't yet been found by another miner. After reading through the plots is complete, the miners' hardware can become idle until the next block. The plot reading process generally does not take long and varies*

112

according to the total size of plots a miner owns."

Next, the agent asked if miners should begin considering the proof-of-capacity scheme to be a realistic venture as opposed to the proof-of-work scheme.

A member of the Burst nation said that it was obvious that the POC should be considered because the whole BURST mining procedure used "off-the-shelf hardware." More importantly, the scheme itself resists ASIC.

He added that the mining process conserves a lot of energy because the modern disk drives are quiet and run on low power, which normally would consume no more than 10 watts during operations. He said that when such an advantage is compared to the heat, noise and power consumption of ASICs or graphic cards used in the process of mining other altcoins, BURST's edge is clear. These features, according to the Burst personnel, enhance the network's decentralization.

The Bitcoinist agent asked if the Burst team could explain the differences between BURST and its close competitor, which he described as "Storj."

A respondent from the Burst team replied that Storj and BURST, at that point in time, were actually not similar at all. He said that Storj's focus was on producing a decentralized drop box which would employ hard drive spaces. He also said that the coin itself was not mined; instead, it was given out according to the amount of hard drive space users gave the network. The respondent also mentioned that Storj's coins are a program on the Mastercoin blockchain application, which means the currency does not allow a personal blockchain. BURST, on the other hand, is mined on hard drive spaces through "plotting" of the hard drives. The plotted space is turned into "hashpower," which is how the coins are generated.

He said, *"Right now BURST is not making use of the hard drive space other than to create power for mining the coin and securing the blockchain.*

"BURST has its own blockchain. BURST will eventually be making use of the space as well, so it will be like Storj with the added benefits of having its own blockchain, and will actually MINE the coin on hard drive space."

The respondent said that the theories behind each altcoin's creation may be close to the surface, but are usually very distinct in reality. He said that BURST's focus is on mining with hard drive spaces as well as getting the best out of their asset exchange, decentralized marketplace and recently initiated ATs, which was a new program other altcoins had been seeking to create but had not been able to accomplish.

He said, *"Like I mentioned though, BURST WILL have storage on the plotted space eventually, as it is on the roadmap. At that point there will still be many differences between the two coins, but they will both have the ability to store files. As of right now the coins are essentially different in almost every way."*

To close the questioning, the Bitcoinist correspondent asked if actual demand existed for a decentralized form of file sharing and, if so, why the Burst team believed this was so.

A member of the Burst team replied, *"I believe if someone is looking for a reason for decentralized file storage, they need to look no further than the recent celebrity picture hacks that took place last summer. Celebrities' private pictures were exposed to the general public because their files were stored in a central location. This central location makes it easier for "hackers" to focus their efforts on one target and gain access to private material. If those files were stored on a decentralized system, there is nothing to "hack" as there is no central storage location to gain access to."*

He said that in a decentralized cloud, users' files are divided into chunks and then dispersed throughout the cloud. That the single medium to hijack the files would have access to the private keys is the same as having access to the password of a centralized network or system.

He also said that in a decentralized system, there is just one way to hijack files, also known as stealing the keys. On the other hand, a centralized system would cause the hijacking of keys and even a system overhaul to occur in the network. He ended his clarification by saying, *"I look forward to the future of a decentralized cloud. I will worry about keeping track of my key, I no longer have to worry about someone else keeping track of the door. Decentralized file storage is yet another proof that Bitcoin has multifaceted applications in the real world. With coins like Burst, more people are benefiting from the advantages cryptography can provide."*

CHAPTER 11: EMERCOIN (EMC)

Launched in December 2013, Emercoin is an open-source cryptocurrency which shares some similarities with Peercoin and Namecoin. These similarities stem from its use of the proof-of-work and proof-of-stake algorithms. It also uses the SHA-256 hash. Beyond a digital currency, Emercoin developers see the Emercoin platform as a network for many other financial services.

A lead developer once said, *"[The] key difference in Emercoin from other cryptocurrencies is that we are using blockchain not just for transfer[ing] credit values. We consider Emercoin as a technological platform for distributed, censorship-proof and scalable services. So we developed a suite of services running on top of the Emercoin blockchain that will be very useful for a lot of companies and even private persons."*

Between 2013 and 2016, several developmental tasks were carried out within the Emercoin platform. By 2016, the following were some of the numerous services integrated into the platform.

Emerboard: Distributed BBS

EMCTTS: A certified store for timestamps on the blockchain

MAGNET: A BitTorrent tracker for online file sharing

EMCDPO: A profound solution for proof of ownership

INFOCARD: A store for e-business cards in the network

EMCDNS: An uncensored domain name which peers with OpenNIC. The OpenNIC is made of servers that provide solutions to issues on Emercoin domains.

THE ANNALS OF EMERCOIN

As mentioned earlier, Emercoin was launched in December 2013. In 2014, sponsorship projects for the cryptocurrency began. Subsequently, subdomains were allowed to operate within Emercoin's server.

Soon afterward, in November, a fork was created in Emercoin's blockchain due to malware attacks from a hack. By December 2015, all loopholes within the blockchain had been fixed and operations began once more.

In January 2016, Emercoin partnered with Microsoft. After that, Emercoin's blockchain was launched in the Azuri market. Other developments included the release of the Emercoin wallet, which is occasionally updated. In the same month, Emercoin was rated one of the best cryptocurrencies in the world.

Emercoin's developers have made it clear that the network's vision transcends the creation of a cryptocurrency. Instead, the Emercoin platform seeks to create an avenue for online transactions whose medium of payment would not be restricted to Emercoins. This vision has taken different forms in terms of various activities the Emercoin team carries out. For instance, the team was able to start a mining company which utilizes EMCSSH. The Hashcoins Company is known to have utilized Emercoin's SSH.

A group of digital currency enthusiasts, Forklog, conducted an in-depth interview with Emercoin's CTO, Nikolai Pavlovski. The following are excerpts from the interview.

The interviewer asked Pavlovski how he began using Emercoin services and how they had helped him. Pavlovski said the early stages began in 2015. Stanislav Polozov of Emercoin had called him to explain the network's abilities. Initially he had thought it would be just another fork, one out of millions. By the time he had a discussion with the developers, he understood how genuine and interesting the platform was.

The interviewer asked when exactly this had happened and what work his organization was involved in at that point in time. Pavlovski said that HashCoins was launched in 2013 and in 2014 his organization began selling equipment for mining. Mining equipment sales were their main business back then. The biggest problem then was that a hardware product cost about $5,000 to $6,000 and not many individuals could afford to buy them. Thereafter, he decided that his company had to attract those with small incomes or limited resources. The organization created HashFlare, a service that allowed an amount less than five dollars. Furthermore, Pavlovski said that the idea was about selling out the capacity of the hardware and not the hardware itself.

He concluded his explanation by stressing that his organization had not only successfully installed an Emercoin wallet inside a miner but had also used the SSH and SSL technologies to ensure that nobody would be able to enter the interface with the use of the Emercoin certificate and equally run internal management with the EmcSSH. He believed that it was a three-in-one solution. Miners worked solo–that is, they worked independently and not in a pool. Users could connect if they wanted to. In addition, it had an Emercoin wallet within it. He remarked that it was very convenient. Nobody had heard about Emercoin at the time. Pavlovski said the difficulty level was somewhat low, making the mining process an easy one.

The Forklog correspondent asked why Pavlovski had originally decided that he needed the EmcSSH technological program. Pavlovski said that if there was just a single miner, there would be no serious problems. The miner could even choose to mine using what is known as the classical method. This meant the miner would create a few keys, after which the miner would store them in a correct folder before connecting to the server. Pavlovski said that when there are so many miners with a huge number of operations staff in the network, some of the miners may have the same location as a user's home. Thus, the problem of proper administration comes up. Pavlovski said his organization had many employees who could access the particular hardware. Some of these employees may quit somewhere along the line and some may get sick. Others could use the knowledge they gained at Emercoin to work for other businesses.

He said, *"So the problem of SSH access is quite frequent. Emercoin solved this problem in a pretty elegant way. Generally, the solution is about linking a public key to a user and sending it to the blockchain. In crude terms, it happens like that. I open the wallet, make an entry that says, SSH is Nicky Pavlovski, and his key is like that."*

The interviewer from Forklog asked whether each employee required such records. Nikolai said each user could publish their public key through their Emercoin wallet. Because he was the company's administrator, Pavlovski could unify the users in groups through the blockchain program.

Pavlovski then provided an example. He said, *"We make a HashCoins group that specifies the users that may access servers. At server side, I just have to specify the group, and then all its members may freely enter without having to enter a password.*

"If somebody quits for instance, a Pete, then myself, being the head admin, I would just update a blockchain record through the wallet and remove the Pete from the group. So, I have no need to enter each server and manually change everything.

We had a situation that required Oleg Khovayko's assistance. So I just added him to our group when needed and removed him when the job was done. It's a pretty convenient technology. Now we use EmcSSH wherever possible."

The interviewer asked if this was expensive.

Pavlovski said the cost was next to nothing, and all costs were incurred in the process of installing an Emercoin wallet. A year before then, programmers had to put together a wallet for every architecture in a process which took about an hour. Pavlovski said that as of the time of the interview, the process had become more convenient, taking just a few minutes. A typical administrator with a small or medium organization would have completed the installation within 10 or so minutes. All expenses were centered on obtaining a junky computer that could adequately and seamlessly run the wallet.

Pavlovski also said users had to make payments for every action or process.

The Forklog contributor asked Pavlovski why only a few organizations have employed and explored Emercoin's program and services. Pavlovski admitted that at the time he started the organization, the situation was a bit complicated. He and other co-workers had to figure out how it worked. The process involved installation as well as learning what it was about. However, recently the situation had become different.

He said that comprehensive papers and corresponding solutions are available. As of the time of the interview, the situation had become simpler and clearer. He was convinced that the need for blockchain technology in general has grown. Furthermore, the entrance limit had been lowered significantly and even regular users could attempt it by themselves without any assistance from Emercoin. He ended by saying that he believed Emercoin services would continue developing and becoming more popular.

Afterwards, his interviewer asked whether similar organizations provide the kinds of solutions that Emercoin does.

Pavlovski said that he believed no existing program could successfully compete with the capabilities of Emercoin and its innovative services. Emercoin is very much ahead of the game in many areas and no one wants to even venture into becoming an alternative to Emercoin. When Emercoin came forward with the news of its technological advancement, many people refused to believe it because several similar proclamations had been made around the same time and had ultimately resulted in nothing specific.

WALLETS

Emercoin payments become instantly possible once a user generates an address for their wallet. These addresses are secured with keys, and every participant needs their key to send or receive Emercoins. Emercoin wallets store addresses and cryptographic keys, which help transfer the coins. Provisions such as access to advanced packages within the network, full control of the Emercoins held in it and the absence of third parties in the process of securing users' private keys are only a few of the privileges that users enjoy when they use Emercoin-based wallets.

This also implies that Emercoin users are fully responsible for keeping their coins safe. The wallets are available on all operating systems, which means they can be downloaded and installed on computer systems or smartphones.

In addition to custom wallets, users have many other wallet options. However, many activities within these other wallets are controlled by their developers or administrators. Users are therefore advised to conduct adequate research before they sign up for external wallets.

HOW TO ACQUIRE EMERCOINS

Users can purchase Emercoins from online exchange platforms. Already, multiple platforms exist where cryptocurrency enthusiasts can exchange their coins. Another way to acquire Emercoins is to accept them as a medium of payment for services the user has rendered. In addition, Emercoins can be acquired by mining.

THE USABILITY OF EMERCOIN

Emercoin can be used to pay for services rendered and for goods purchased by its users. It is one of the leading cryptocurrencies currently available. Many online platforms already accept it. Technological advancements in the Emercoin platform have broadened the opportunities available to those who possess the coin.

Because of its extra security options and diverse functions in terms of dealing with the management of payments, Emercoin has great prospects, for both individuals and businesses across the globe.

DECENTRALIZATION OF DOMAIN NAMES

Users are given the room to modify transfers and change their domain names within the network. This means no third party or developer can tamper with a user's domain name. Also, these domain names are securely stored using personal cryptographic keys. Currently, OpenNIC works hand in hand with Emercoin domains.

Decentralization in Emercoin also extends to its blockchain.

Advanced programs such as Digitalstamps, EMCSSL and management programs for administrators are already functioning within the Emercoin blockchain. These programs give users more room to productively use the blockchain.

INTERESTS

On a yearly basis, holders can earn as much as six percent interest due to Emercoin's proof-of-stake mechanism. In essence, this implies that once a user who has stored coins in Emercoin's custom wallet leaves it open for the minting process, the user can earn an additional six percent of their coins after a year.

CHAPTER 12: PUTINCOIN

PutinCoin revolves around the Russian president, Vladimir Putin. While the currency's name stems from that of the president, it was invented to commend and emphasize the Russian economy, whose buoyancy is a result of Putin's hard work as described by many of his loyal citizens. As in Peercoin, PutinCoin uses two algorithms. The use of these two algorithms sets PutinCoin apart from many other cryptocurrencies.

BENEFITS OF PUTINCOIN

PutinCoin is used in different sectors and establishments. It can be used by financial institutions, traders and private individuals. This cross-sector feature makes PutinCoin a flexible cryptocurrency that anyone around the world can use. Plans are already being made to ensure that PutinCoin will offer solutions to payment difficulties that individuals and businesses experience. Currently, many wallets are in PutinCoin's network. With PutinCoin, users do not need to move around with physical currencies, as anyone around the world can access the platform.

SECURITY

Through use of the scrypt algorithm and encryption, the security of transactions in Peercoin's blockchain is guaranteed. The proof-of-work and proof-of-stake algorithms give the system a hybrid structure. The transfer and receipt of PutinCoin are securely processed using a comprehensive algorithm. This means that operations within the network are free from malware and hackers. Also, the proof-of-work and proof-of-stake algorithms ensure that no third party has control over its operations. Transactions are completely anonymous.

THE PUTINCOIN TECHNOLOGY

Users of PutinCoin do not need complex hardware to carry out transactions or to mine. The proof-of-stake mechanism is readily available on many computer systems. Furthermore, a 100 percent mining interest is provided on a yearly basis. With its technology, only authorized individuals can gain access to transactions and general information on its blockchain.

DECENTRALIZATION

PutinCoin is a completely decentralized cryptocurrency, as it has no central control or location where transactions are recorded. Transactions within PutinCoin's blockchain do not have a specified origin or destination. They simply flow across all the systems connected to the platform. Its decentralized features also give users access to their coins whenever and wherever they need them. Users also do not need to be in any particular physical location to retrieve their coins.

DEVELOPMENT

Since PutinCoin's introduction, its growth rate has been above average. Also, investments in the currency are said to yield high interest over time. To facilitate the supply and continuous growth of PutinCoin, its developers plan to integrate it into every exchange platform currently on the network. Just like Auroracoin, PutinCoin is a nationally championed cryptocurrency.

CHAPTER 13: PEERCOIN (PPC)

Peercoin is a digital currency which uses the proof-of-work and proof-of-stake algorithms. In a white paper published in August 2012, Scott Nadal and Sunny King were listed as the cryptocurrency's core developers. Soon after, Nadal withdrew himself from the platform. This ultimately enthroned King as the sole developer of Peercoin.

"Peercoin seeks to be the most secure cryptocoin at the lowest cost, rewarding all users for strengthening the network by giving them a 1% annual PPC return when minting." – Peercoin's official website

Several codes present within Peercoin's network are direct duplicates of Bitcoin's mechanisms. These codes are broadcast through the MIT software license. Peercoin's distinctive feature is the fact that the cryptocurrency does not have a limited number of currencies to be mined. It is otherwise programmed to have an inflation rate of one percent at the end of every year. Inflation is controlled through 0.01 PPC per kilobyte, which represents a transaction fee within the platform. This fee is destroyed as soon as a transaction has been completed. This destruction process not only creates a medium for the control of yearly inflation, but also ensures that the cryptocurrency remains scalable. Peercoin transactions are moderated by a peer-to-peer network on its blockchain. This means that balances are processed through the SHA-256 proof-of-work scheme.

Currently, exchanges from and to bitcoins, some other cryptocurrencies as well as a few fiat currencies are possible with Peercoin. However, these exchanges are essentially conducted online. Also, Peercoin transactions are usually not reversible, which means chargebacks are not available on the platform. According to its developers, "Peercoin" is an abridged version of "peer-to-peer coin transactions."

Addresses in the Peercoin network consist of 34 numbers and letters that usually start with the letter P. These sets of figures and letters are based on digital signatures. Only through these addresses can payments can be made within the platform. Without any cost or charge, users can create multiple addresses in the system.

To a large extent, users of Peercoin use single addresses for single purposes or transactions. All transactions on the network are documented in a ledger, also known as the Peercoin blockchain. Every 10 minutes, new blocks are added to the blockchain. After an estimated 60 minutes, transactions are considered to have been completed after the sixth block.

CREATION/ MINING OF PEERCOINS

Peercoin cryptocurrency can be created through two procedures: mining and minting. While the minting process gifts coins in relation to the number of Peercoins users hold, mining uses the SHA-256 algorithm. *"Proof of Work mining is used to spread the distribution of new coins, while the security of the network is maintained entirely by Proof of Stake minting. This means that Bitcoin mining vulnerabilities such as Selfish Mining do not impact Peercoin's security."*- Peercoin's official website.

PROTECTION OF PEERCOIN

Peercoin's developers have suggested that the system would depend more on minting in the future. Not only would the dependability lead to rewards, it would ensure a fair distribution of coins within the system.

DISTINGUISHING FEATURES

The combination of the proof-of-work and the proof-of-stake algorithms is an outstanding feature of Peercoin which makes it unique among several cryptocurrencies. Because a system which thrives on only the proof-of-work system could be exposed to double spending and other misappropriations, the proof-of-stake algorithm was infused in the network to serve as a backup to the proof-of-work mechanism. The proof-of-stake algorithm enables the creation of new coins using the number of coins users hold. The creation of one percent of every proof-of-stake block corresponds to another one percent of the currency a user holds. With this sort of mechanism, monopolizing the transactions and activities in the Peercoin network becomes very expensive.

Since the entire Peercoin network uses the SHA-256 algorithm, rewards for the proof-of-work block are divided in two after the 16th increase within the network.

FEATURES

An excerpt from Peercoin's whitepaper adequately describes what Peercoin has to offer. It reads: *"Proof-of-work helped to give birth to Nakamoto's major breakthrough. However, the nature of proof-of-work means that the cryptocurrency is dependent on energy consumption. Thus, introducing significant cost overhead in the operation of such networks is borne by the users via a combination of inflation and transaction fees. As the mint rate slows in the Bitcoin network, eventually it could put pressure on increasing transaction fees to sustain a preferred level of security. One naturally asks whether we must maintain energy consumption in order to have a decentralized cryptocurrency?"*

Therefore, this cryptocurrency has been a significant

advancement in both theory and technological application in terms of showing that the consumption of excess energy is not necessarily important for the adequate security and protection of digital currencies.

REDUCED ENERGY CONSUMPTION

Since it was discovered that Bitcoin consumes power, causing the expenditure of a significant amount of resources to regulate its network every day, Peercoin developers decided to include the proof of stake. This was to ensure that the system conserves energy. Once the proof-of-stake algorithm is used to create coins, it would essentially be run on a computer. This is unlike Bitcoin's algorithm, which must run heavy cryptographic hash functions.

The idea of unlimited mining will ensure the continuous flow of Peercoins in the exchange market. Already, a total of 20.7 million Peercoins are in circulation, and this number is set to increase over time. In addition, value might be preserved through Peercoin's regulation of the currency's flow in the exchange market. Once users recognize Peercoin as a valuable cryptocurrency, it becomes more viable for use in transactions.

THE INFLATION MECHANISM

The possibility of having an unlimited number of Peercoin in circulation is seen through its proposed yearly inflation of one percent. The idea to create a platform with an unlimited number of coins in its community is meant address the possibility of incrementing in Peercoin's population.

As mentioned earlier, a 0.01 PPC per kilobyte fee is charged for every transaction within Peercoin's platform. These fees do not end up with miners or anyone within the network; instead, they are destroyed upon a transaction's completion. The transaction fee's principal purpose is to regulate the Peercoin inflation rate. It is also believed that transaction fees curb different forms of spam that could possibly arise in the network. Furthermore, the transaction fee is fixed permanently. It does not increase or decrease at any point even when the Peercoin value changes.

"The joint mechanisms of 1% annual interest and 0.01 PPC commission creates a particularly interesting dynamic from which Peercoin is primarily designed to discourage frequent transactions and encourage its possession. This feature makes Peercoin uninteresting as a payment platform, making its purpose significantly different from the other currencies that are certainly more transaction-friendly." – DigitalGain

BEYOND ONLINE PLATFORMS

A remark on "heavy.com" remarked on Peercoin's achievement beyond its online community. It reads: *"Peercoin is the Official Money at a Star Trek Convention Called Trek Con, being held in May in Springfield, Missouri; Peercoin is being accepted for tickets, merchandise, and anything that can be found at the convention."*

With Peercoin, the probability that a few users will control activities in the network is minimal. This is because its proof-of-stake algorithm was programmed to ensure that monopolization is essentially impossible. No doubt, should Peercoin continue following the paths of its mechanisms and ideas, it can successfully compete against Bitcoin. In the not-so-distant future, Peercoin is bound to become a genuine and viable cryptocurrency. King, Peercoin's core developer, ensured that he researched Bitcoin's major flaws and weaknesses and improved on them significantly. This improvement has boosted the digital currency's reliability.

MINTING PEERCOIN

A wallet, widely referred to as the hot wallet, must be properly connected to Peercoin's network to mint new coins. This wallet is constantly exposed to malware because it must be connected to the network throughout the minting process. Because it has become a main focus of concern, an update is planned to address this loophole. The update will enable users to keep their wallets offline during the minting process.

Peercoin's blockchain allows transactions to be processed within milliseconds. A block explorer immediately validates payment. The fast process of conducting and confirming transactions makes it impossible for users to reverse any transaction that has been conducted.

CHAPTER 14: AURORACOIN (AUR)

In 2014, an anonymous developer from Iceland launched a cryptocurrency named Auroracoin. It is a form of peer-to-peer digital currency which serves as an alternative to Bitcoin and the Icelandic national currency, krona. It was created by some pseudonymous figure(s) commonly referred to as Baldur Friggjar Odinsson. Auroracoin's creation was intended to stem the financial crisis in which Icelanders had found themselves.

Fifty percent of the pre-mined digital currency was to be distributed to all Icelanders, which is about 330,000 people. This meant that every citizen registered in the country's database was entitled approximately 31.8 Auroracoin each.

Before Auroracoin's introduction, the country's government had restricted the movement of krona outside the country. Therefore, Auroracoin received the same treatment when it was launched. That policy automatically branded Auroracoin as one of the first country-based cryptocurrencies. It could be used only for transactions within the country.

THE ANNALS OF AURORACOIN

The United States was not the only country affected by the 2008 financial crisis. The consequences of that economic collapse had adverse effects on the economies of many countries around the world, and Iceland was no exception. Just before the country was hit with the economic meltdown, Iceland had been thriving due to Range Rovers being sold in different countries. However, the crisis caused a massive devaluation of Iceland's national currency. The effect of those ugly events was devastating; all residents became victims of panic and chaos into the country. In turn, executives and officers of financial institutions were jailed after being found liable for the nationwide crisis.

Eventually, Iceland's residents began to pick up the pieces from the ruins of the economic collapse. They sought to fix the country's bruised economy through patriotism and nationalistic acts. After a series of trials and considerations, an anonymous developer came up with the idea of creating another form of currency, one that would serve as an alternative to krona, with the goal of rescuing the nation from its devastation and crushed economy. This currency would be computer-based.

As expected, not everyone believed that an alternative digital currency was the solution to the country's financial crisis. Instead, the currency was seen as a way to ensure that the dependability of physical financial institutions would decrease. Also, its introduction represented an experiment with a new form of financial transaction. No doubt, Bitcoin's success in other countries influenced Auroracoin's invention.

Auroracoin is based on Norse mythology, with references to Baldor, Frigg and Odin. Although Auroracoin's mechanism is based largely on Bitcoin's protocol, it also employs the proof-of-work algorithm found in the Litecoin cryptocurrency.

THE SPREAD OF AURORACOIN

As mentioned earlier, 31.8 Auroracoins were initially proposed to be distributed to each of Iceland's registered residents, totaling 320,000 beneficiaries. At the time it was released, an Auroracoin was equal to $12. That meant each recipient would receive an amount equal to $385. Soon after, Auroracoin's value dropped. After the drastic devaluation, 636 Auroracoins were distributed. By then, citizens were no longer convinced about its prospects. They instantly lost confidence in the digital currency, claiming it would never live up to its expectations.

FEATURES

Upon its launch, Auroracoin was based on Litecoin's proof-of-work algorithm. However, subsequent versions of its blockchain used a multi-algorithm architecture based on DigiByte's algorithm. Furthermore, transactions within Auroracoin's network are irreversible. This means no third party can restrict or control any transaction within the platform. It is a strict peer-to-peer form of transaction which no external individual can infiltrate. On the other hand, users cannot complain to anyone about incomplete or unsuccessful transactions.

NO GUARANTEE OF ANONYMITY: Auroracoin's ledger is a public blockchain which allows users to identify transactions made by other participants. While some exchange markets offer a mixing mechanism that helps achieve privacy during Auroracoin transactions, it is complex. Therefore, to achieve a form of privacy when transacting with Auroracoin, new addresses should be generated for every transaction.

THE AIRDROP

The process of distributing Auroracoins to Iceland's citizens was tagged the "airdrop." Through its distribution, the anonymous developer intended to expose the world of digital currency to every member of the country.

The first phase, which was initiated in March 2014, saw the distribution of about 281,000 coins on the first day. Upon the completion of the first phase in July 2014, a total of 1,126,674 Auroracoins had been distributed to 35,430 residents. That meant that after the first phase, about 300,000 residents had been left out of the distribution process. The second phase, which ran from July to November of the same year, recorded the distribution of 1.6 million coins to 5,024 residents. At the time, the value of Auroracoin had fallen significantly, causing an increment in the amount of Auroracoins distributed. The initial 31.8 coins were increased to 318 coins. Two thousand six hundred residents were able to claim 1.7 million Auroracoins at end of the third phase, which was conducted from November 2014 to March 2015.

The value of Auroracoin continued to decrease, meaning that the number of coins given to beneficiaries had to be increased. Six hundred and thirty-six Auroracoins were distributed during the project's third phase. At the program's conclusion, 5,344,628 Auroracoins were "burned" to make them inaccessible. It was said that the aforementioned coins were not claimed by their intended recipients

THE AURORACOIN FOUNDATION

To improve its technology and to foster Auroracoin's development in Iceland, a foundation for the digital currency was introduced in March 2015. Upon its introduction, Auroracoin's core developer released a total of one million Auroracoins to fund the organization.

USES OF AURORACOIN

A number of Auroracoin wallets are available on the App store and Google Play. There are also various computer-based wallets for Auroracoin users. However, it is recommended that IOS users use the Hiveweb wallet, while Android users are advised to use the Coinomi wallet on their smartphones. In addition, computer or paper wallets are ideal for the storage of large amounts of Auroracoins. Once the user has acquired the wallet, passwords and security keys must be adequately stored.

TRANSFER AND RECEPTION OF AURORACOINS AS A PAYMENT OPTION

A user can accept Auroracoins in their wallet after they have sent an address to the sending party. The address is readily available on the user's wallet. The user must simply copy the address and send it to the other party. Once the address has been received, the sender will transfer the required amount of the coin to the address they received. The recipient instantly receives a confirmation that a specific amount of the coin has been sent to their wallet address.

WAYS TO ACQUIRE AURORACOIN

Auroracoin can be exchanged for the Icelandic currency, krona. Also, bitcoins can be exchanged for Auroracoins. That is, a user can exchange their bitcoins for an equivalent value of Auroracoins. Selling physical items and getting paid with Auroracoins is another way in which Auroracoins can be acquired.

THE DEVELOPMENT OF AURORACOIN

Petur Amarson is among the first set of residents who tapped into the mining of Auroracoin. Along with others, he had seen that mining cryptocurrencies could help prevent financial disasters like that which occurred in 2008. He continued his efforts to create a level of importance for cryptocurrencies, and his efforts led to the introduction of an exchange platform for cryptocurrencies in Iceland. Beyond the creation of a viable cryptocurrency, Amarson recognized the need for computer technicians and programmers in the country. He discovered an opportunity to develop the country's capability in its technology sector and in the cryptocurrency revolution.

He once said: *"Our main focus has always been to get people to adopt the coin. If you get enough people using the coin you will get more people to develop and improve the coin and ecosystem. This is, however, the opposite of what most other coins are doing. They are focusing the majority of their efforts on improving the technology in the hope that the new technology will drive adoption. I believe this to be the wrong approach."*

Amarson also said, *"I think adoption will drive the technology advancement of the coin."*

Therefore, Amarson tried to take advantage of his belief that Auroracoin was the way out of the county's financial woes. However, he realized that the currency was not gaining the recognition he had envisioned. Its reliability was a source of mixed reactions. In addition, the currency had no exchange platform. Many traders refused to accept it as a medium of exchange, believing its value could not be equated with fiat currencies, especially krona.

Despite the increasing rejection of the cryptocurrency, Amarson continued to sensitize and convince Icelanders to become involved in the coin's exchange and use. In the long run, the initial struggles to convince residents to participate yielded positive results. Amarson was able to create a forum in which developmental talks about Auroracoin were constantly held. Afterwards, the anonymous inventor of the coin ejected himself from the system. He wanted users to have total control over the platform's activities.

The forum's success, which Amarson created, ultimately led to the creation of the Auroracoin Foundation. Since then, Auroracoin has gone through one development after another. The foundation has carried out awareness programs and developmental tasks using one million Auroracoins that were released upon its establishment.

The team that has ensured the advancement of Auroracoin includes Craig Dellandrea, Hermann I. Finnbjornsson, Hlynur Bjornsson, Jess Foddrill, Martin Jansen, Myckel Habets, Petur Arnason, Tom Hendriks and Yan Crevier.

CHAPTER 15: NXT (NXT)

Nxt is an open-source cryptocurrency with advanced structures that can be traced to Bitcoin. It was introduced in November 2013. Apart from its own digital currency, other programs such as a marketplace, a voting system, decentralized assets, account control, coin shuffling, data cloud, alias system, messaging, monetary system and others are the outstanding features or programs within the Nxt network. This means users can create forums for marketing and make payments without any restrictions.

"The designers of Nxt have set their sights not just on creating a viable currency, but on fostering an entire fiscal ecosystem online. Nxt has the technology to back up this lofty goal and already boasts a significant user base, but whether it becomes the community of choice for online exchange remains to be seen." – Toptenreviews

Also, through the application program feature, developers have the room to write applications. The network has a stable flow of transactions due to its use of the proof-of-stake algorithm. More importantly, it features a multi-signature program, as seen in the NEM cryptocurrency. The Nxt digital currency can be used for transactions within and outside the platform. It is also used to represent assets.

THE ANNALS OF NXT

After a successful fundraising program on Bitcointalk, Nxt was launched on November 24, 2013. Its first-ever block was created the same day. Afterwards, 73 participants were able to get one billion coins. Those one billion Nxt coins were shared according to the rate of each participant's investment in the fundraising event. Under the MIT license, the full source code for Nxt launched in March 2014.

FEATURES

In Nxt's network, blocks are created within one minute. Furthermore, the platform is written in Java, which makes it easy to operate from any internet-enabled system. Nxt is also the first digital currency to exclusively use the proof-of-stake algorithm for its consensus.

Bitcoin.com had a concise interview with Dave Pearce, one of the founders of the Nxt foundation. The details are as follows:

Bitcoin.com's correspondent asked about Pearce's thoughts on LZF's decision to bring a Nxt/USD pair to the public. He asked if the co-founder was anticipating major interest in Nxt, as direct trading against some fiat currencies had become possible.

Pearce said it was always good news whenever he heard about a new marketplace for Nxt, and that even though LZF was still somehow "under the radar" for many Nxt community members, Nxt did have a few exchanges through Nxt fiat markets. The exchange was already possible on CCEDK (NXT EUR+), as well as on BTC38 (NXT CNY). Pearce said exchanges are also available through several brokers, including Litebit and Coinimal. Again, he said that his expectation was that the listing would be a positive step forward for Nxt. He then said that LZF seemed like a good and standard organization but he didn't think it was a groundbreaking story.

The interviewer mentioned that Nxt had sponsored some notable events with a company known as Reinvent. He said that money was involved in a recent event. The interviewer then asked that with Pearce being a developer, what that type of publicity meant to him. The interviewer also asked whether, during évents, Pearce tried to provide particular information about the platform's progress or whether the events were purely promotional.

Pearce said that in many of the events, especially the one at Reinvent Money, the target audience was varied. The most important information to get across to people was general information about what cryptocurrency was, the meaning of Nxt and particularly, the way or ways in which Nxt could be used.

Pearce said that the 1.7 release would contain many interesting features, such as a coin-shuffling system.

The interviewer asked Pearce what Nxt would do to make the platform the topic of popular discussion in the following year.

Pearce said he was tied to the setup of multiple elements of the Tennessee project, which included a new emphasis on marketing and PR, as well as plans to make the Nxt user experience as pleasant as possible. A giant step he and his team members were taking on the project was to establish a helpdesk service for Nxt users. The program would go live before the end of that particular year.

Finally, Pearce said, *"On the development front, the 1.7 release will bring a lot of interesting features, including a coin shuffling system. We've just completed a review of the Shuffling system with Tim Ruffing (originator of the Coin Shuffle system for BTC), and he is happy with the Nxt implementation.*

"There's going to be a lot more, including several magazine/book releases that will give us some great tools to explain and promote Nxt to the more mainstream world, not just inside the crypto scene."

VOTING SYSTEM

Nxt's successful, decentralized voting system proves that cryptographic platforms can be used in elections. Crowdfunding and the development of programs by other developers are just a few of the advantages that Nxt enjoys through its plugin feature.

MONETARY PROGRAM

The monetary program creates room for the production of digital currencies on the blockchain, although their value is relative to a certain amount of the Nxt currency itself.

PROOF OF STAKE

Nxt's use of proof of stake eliminates some risks present in other cryptocurrencies. The proof-of-stake scheme also requires less hashing power.

TRANSPARENT FORGING

Nxt includes a feature called transparent forging, which reduces the transaction rate to a level that other cryptocurrencies can rarely match. Because users can determine the node that will generate a new block, transactions from other nodes can easily be transferred to such nodes. Transparent forging also includes a security measure which protects the system against forgeries.

ACCESSIBILITY

Developers have room to increase Nxt's functionality of Nxt by making the API open and accessible to anyone.

THE NXT BLOCKCHAIN

The Nxt blockchain is an integral feature of the Nxt

cryptocurrency. This is because developers and users can easily integrate the blockchain into their personal projects or programs.

With the simple API, transactions are automatically decentralized, secure and reliable. Also, because the opportunity exists for developers and users in general to create applications, crowdfunding, governing programs as well as financial programs are constantly being conducted within the network.

COMMUNITY

The Nxt platform already has a community of about 100,000 members; that number continues to increase due to the cryptocurrency's growing popularity.

CIRCULATION

Nxt was not mined. All its units were given to 73 stakeholders upon its launch through Bitcointalk.

CHAPTER 16: MONERO (XMR)

While many cryptocurrencies are associated with Bitcoin, Monero is among the few altcoins that has proven such categorizations to be wrong. Formally launched in 2014, Monero is an open-source digital currency whose strengths are its scalability, privacy and decentralization. With its distinct algorithm and CryptoNote domain, Monero sets itself apart from the hundreds of cryptocurrencies currently in circulation. Its unique mechanisms and processes quickly attracted the interest of AlphaBay, a popular digital currency market, which in turn boosted its market capitalization in 2016. Monero offers solutions to the vital privacy constraints that Bitcoin experiences.

Dash is another platform that offers privacy, although critics consider its technique of mixing up transactions to ensure anonymity to be substandard. Also, Zcash's advanced security mechanism has yet to be fully integrated into prominent markets.

A supplement to Monero's fluid cryptocurrency is its standard anonymity feature. Encrypted addresses are generated to transfer Monero through an innovative technique known as "stealth addresses." Stealth addresses prevent transactions within the network from being traced.

"The stealth address feature is a huge upgrade over Bitcoin's privacy. Here's the best way to think of it... With bitcoin, you reveal your real "home address" in order to send and receive bitcoin. With Monero, you use the equivalent of a "post office box" as your address to send and receive Monero. By using a virtual P.O. Box instead of your actual address, your transactions cannot be linked back to you." – Steemit

Furthermore, through another technique, called "ring

signatures," a sender's address is merged into a group of many other addresses within Monero's network.

"A ring signature is a way to make sure a transaction can't be tied back to a specific individual. Think about this example...

"Imagine a million hundred dollar notes with a thousand fingerprints on each note. It would be impossible to tie the note to a single person. As you transact through the network, it mixes the public information of hundreds of transactions together. (Your money is still yours. It's never commingled with anyone else's.)

"A $100 bill with 100 sets of fingerprints on it and yours is one of those sets. There's no way anyone can tie that $100 bill back to you. That's how ring signatures work. With each transaction, digital fingerprints (called signatures) are attached to the transaction... effectively making it impossible for anyone to conclusively prove that the transaction came from you." – Steemit

And to cap its amazing privacy features, even the amounts of transactions are hidden through the "ring confidential transactions" program. In addition, subsequent updates of the Monero platform will feature I2P software which will hide internet traffic during transactions.

With all these cutting-edge features, Monero is a viable cryptocurrency with a promising future.

THE ANNALS OF MONERO

Nicolas van Saberhagen was the first name to ever be tagged with Monero, although this name is largely considered a pseudonym. Van Saberhagen published a white paper which was then referred to as CryptoNote. Soon after its release, another anonymous developer, "thankful for today," transformed van Saberhagen's ideas into a digital currency named Bitmonero. Some developers criticized "thankful for today's" protocol, saying its features were impracticable. Eventually, Bitmonero was transformed into Monero. (In Esperanto, "Monero" means "coin.")

Apart from the faulty substandard codes discovered and addressed, Monero has had two basic improvements. The emission rate from the Bitmonero model was reduced by 50 percent while the target block time was decreased to 60 seconds. After its official launch, a GPU miner based on the proof-of-work algorithm was introduced into the system. The "ring confidential Transactions" introduced in January 2017 marked an important point in Monero's development. Since then, users can opt to conceal the amounts of their transactions.

FEATURES

By 2022, it is expected that a total of 18.4 million Monero coins will have been mined. While the figure is Monero's initial emission curve, subsequent supplementary emissions would begin by May 2022 to retain a form of reward for its miners should the maximum amount of the currency be reached.

PRIVACY

By default, Monero's blockchain is largely opaque compared to other cryptocurrencies not based on the CryptoNote protocol. The "viewkey" opens up a form of transparency in the platform but almost all users employ the privacy features of blockchain. In fact, these features are the principal reasons why users signed up with the platform in the first place.

As mentioned earlier, Monero's core achievement is its provision of advanced privacy mechanisms. Essentially,

Monero's network has three basic features: ring signatures, stealth addresses and ring confidential transactions.

The ring signature feature automatically hides a sender's address, making the source of the transaction untraceable. Stealth addresses protect the recipient's address, which also implies that transactions' destinations are unknown. The ring confidential transaction hides the amounts of transactions within the network. All these privacy options show the complexity of Monero's cryptography and are practiced without any influence or control by third parties or developers. Even miners are not aware of the destination of private transactions within the Monero system. Already, a fourth privacy mechanism is in the works. It aims to prevent the tracing of transaction nodes in I2P. All in all, Monero has been widely regarded as a genuinely interchangeable currency.

UNLINKABLE

To prevent security or privacy leaks, Monero developers invented a protocol that generates a one-time address for every transaction which doesn't appear on its blockchain. Only the recipients have access to these addresses.

SECURE

Monero's wallets are secure. The complex cryptographic mechanisms used to build the wallets make it a herculean task for individuals to tamper with users' funds.

THE MONERO MARKET

Monero's successful privacy techniques extend to its sales on popular markets. The value of Monero immediately increased after Oasis and Alphabay integrated the currency into their platforms.

A downside to its provision of private and secure transactions is its susceptibility to illegal transactions such as those involving drugs and arms dealing. Monero has continuously been criticized about such issues but its developers have said that the advantages it offers in terms of legal transactions outweigh the disadvantages. Hence, the focus should be on its positive usability.

DECENTRALIZATION AND MINING

Decisions about development are very straightforward and are given to the public for discussion. In addition, the developers' meeting logs are uploaded to the public and accessible to every stakeholder.

Monero's smart mining program maintains room for a transparent form of CPU mining on every user's system. It is far from a "de facto" centralization of pool mining, and some mining farms continue to follow Satoshi Nakamoto's original idea of a true peer-to-peer (P2P) currency.

The Cryptonight-based proof-of-work algorithm that Monero had adopted enhances its mining. It also has a smart mining program with a decentralized mining process. Transparent mining through the CPUs of users' computers represents a true implementation of a peer-to-peer currency. The CLI wallet houses the smart mining program for Monero miners across different operating systems.

SUCCINCT EXPLANATION OF MONERO'S IMPORTANT ASPECTS

A question-and-answer session was conducted by a prominent member of the digital currency platform Deepdotweb with "fluffypony," who is one of Monero's core team members. Following are excerpts.

Deepdotweb said that about 70 developers on GitHub had contributed to the project but fluffypony's core team of seven seemed small for a digital currency that was, at the time, in fifth place in relation to its market cap. The correspondent asked if fluffypony felt like Monero's community provided adequate support as well as whether fluffypony was happy with the level of involvement and the current size of the core team. Fluffypony said that the core team members were happy with their level of involvement as well as the project's direction.

He said, *"That being said, we of course are constantly looking for new people to come in and contribute. In terms of the core team, people do come and go, but I think its size should stay the same as its focus is more towards stewardship as opposed to development."*

The interviewer said that Bitcoin was prone to doublespending, a situation that could become a negative issue for 'time-critical' transactions, such as buying a bottle of drink at a restaurant. The correspondent asked if Monero was also prone to double spends. He asked if Monero had the same issues, were there plans in place to make the digital currency a resistant one?

Fluffypony explained that with Bitcoin, if developers wanted to control 50% of the mining network, the programmers could have done whatever they wanted with the inclusion of double spending, which had always been seen as Bitcoin's major weakness. Fluffypony said that if a programmer decided to be involved in doublespending but did not have 50% of the network, they could also participate in a transaction malleability attack which was in turn achieved through the modification of a transaction's signature. This would be done to ensure that it was still valid and thereafter to rebroadcast it.

Fluffypony said, *"Monero has a different malleability attack surface compared to Bitcoin, but that is not to say that we*

149

don't suffer from malleability attacks. To make Monero more resistant to these sorts of attacks, we are looking to add a layer on top of the existing architecture such as TumbleBit or Lightning Network, which are off-blockchain technologies that reduce transaction times."

Afterwards, the interviewer asked if fluffypony thought a single digital currency could prove to be fungible and untraceable, and could be used to conduct instant transactions at the same time, just as physical cash was being used.

Fluffypony said that although much work would have to be carried out, it was absolutely possible to achieve such a landmark. The development was already in motion. He also said that new projects like TumbleBit could be pivotal in the field. TumbleBit was a layer two system capable of making payments instantly without employing too many privacy techniques, as it primarily mixed together all transactions in a decentralized manner.

The correspondent said that Monero's price had been volatile in the months before the interview, possibly due to its adoption in some Dark Net markets like Oasis, which had gone offline, and Alpha Bay. He said that some people had begun to bet on the probability that the cryptocurrency would be Bitcoin's replacement in the Dark Net markets. He asked whether fluffypony believed that would occur.

Fluffypony's said that his gut feeling was no; for many reasons, Bitcoin was sufficient. He said it was not wise to assume that another cryptocoin could sprout from nowhere and take away Bitcoin's throne for no tangible reason.

The correspondent said that according to articles on Monero's official website, non-participants have no way of uncovering the origins, destinations or amounts transacted through Monero within its network. He added that fluffypony and his team were working to improve the way in which transaction amounts are hidden on the network through a process known as "ring confidential transactions" or RingCT for short. Was the development carried out because Monero's current structure could be hacked or was it just a bid to secure the digital currency's future?

Fluffypony said that security was a process and that there would always be new forms of attacks against which the system would need to protect itself. He said it was not advisable for developers to sit by idly and say that they have conclusively solved security issues in a network. Fluffypony said that if a developer said he was done, it would be only a matter of time before he discovered that, in fact, he was not. Developers ask themselves how they can decrease some meta data linkage and time-based attacks, which was obviously an issue whenever they addressed blockchain-related issues. He said that a blockchain contains a lot of data—a considerably large amount for any attacker to process or analyze.

Furthermore, he said, *"Both with Bitcoin and Monero, blockchain is like a Sudoku puzzle and we are making sure the Monero puzzle is significantly larger and thus harder to solve than the Bitcoin puzzle. People come up with interesting ideas of how Monero could be broken (which in turn helps us refine our security) but nobody has come up with a concrete way of breaking Monero."*

The interviewer said he believed the switch to ring confidential transactions would ultimately replace the already-popular ring signatures carved out from the platform's underlying protocol called CryptoNote. The correspondent asked if that was comparable to the process of changing the engine of a car; would fluffypony get nervous due to the possibility that a component could get broken?

Fluffypony said that ring confidential transactions would be an additional form of ring signature; he wasn't planning to move away from the core ring signature which was a substantial part of CrypoNote. The situation could be likened to a hybrid car, which contains a petrol engine in addition to the new electronic form of car fueling. He was not nervous about the possibility of a component breaking, as the developers were sure their mechanisms were robust. Already, RingCT had been released on testnet, which was also a blockchain in a testing environment for some months, and he and other developers had spent a lot of time fiddling with it.

Fluffypony said that they had designed Monero in such a way that if intruding programmers were able to crack one particular mechanism, they would never be able to crack all of them. The mechanism is a great testament to the Monero Research Labs as well as Greg Maxwell, who was responsible for the creation of confidential transactions right from the onset.

Deepdotweb asked whether users were able to use their old wallets, including Hydrogen Helix.

Fluffypony said that this was not possible; users would have to upgrade their accounts so they could use ring confidential transactions. He added that the old nodes could not understand transactions, which could lead to a situation in which such users would be "forked off" from the network. However, the developers would never restrict users from their personal funds.

He said, *"As long as you have access to your wallet file or your 25 word mnemonic seed, you will be able to restore your wallet no matter how far into the future."*

The interviewer asked about the current stage of development for the ring confidential transactions. Fluffypony said it had been completed already and was running on testnet. The ring confidential transactions program is planned to be launched in the near future on Mainnet, which is Monero's principal blockchain.

Fluffypony said he and the other developers had intentionally moved the deadline forward to ensure that users began using the ring confidential transactions early enough. The ring confidential transactions would be optional until September 2017. Thereafter, by December 2017 users must have upgraded to the new version of the Monero application to prevent a negative experience borne out of slow synchronization.

The interviewer said that a popular web wallet, Jaxx, had made plans to add Monero to its already long list of integrated wallets but had failed on many occasions. The correspondent asked if fluffypony could see any significant issues threatening the integration. In addition, he asked whether users would soon be able to hold Monero in their Jaxx wallet.

Fluffypony said he had many dealings with the Jaxx team, who really understood the way Monero works.

The interviewer said that an article on Monero's official website noted that the full Monero client would give users the maximum degree of privacy that Monero could offer as a cryptocurrency. He asked how bad it would be should he choose an alternative to the full client, which meant the user would not run their own node.

Fluffypony said that there would always be privacy breaches if a user had not run their personal nodes. That simply meant that such a user did not download blockchain but still went ahead and ran the wallet application on their computer system. He said that whenever a user employed a third-party wallet, that user would rely on other people for the process of scanning almost all transactions for outputs that originally belonged to the user. The reliance also meant that the other users would have to be in possession of part of the user's private key, also known as the private view key.

The interviewer said that Monero developers had been working tirelessly on a GUI (graphical user interface) whose source code had been released. He asked if any major function of Monero was proving difficult to integrate into the GUI program.

Fluffypony said that at the moment, the basic functions—which were the sending and receiving of transactions as well as synchronizing with the platform—were already present. He said the team did have plans to add more advanced technical functions, such as a smart-mining feature, which was a form of mining and blockchain review process. The feature would be a background to the domain, ultimately protecting the user's processor from a burnout or fault.

The interviewer said that users with inconsistent internet connections would have a hard time trying to download the blockchain. He asked if the new GUI would support remotely positioned nodes, which also meant the leaching of a blockchain already in existence.

Fluffypony said that the GUI would support remote nodes. However, he mentioned that the team was trying to discourage this situation because the stress placed on the remote nodes available for the function would be abnormal. He said the user's level of privacy would be affected in a negative way once the user began using a remote node. Because of the actions the user would be carrying out, the node to which the user connected could entail certain information only for the user's consumption.

The Deepdotweb correspondent asked what damage would

result if he had downloaded the GUI and decided to run his personal node. He said that he wanted to know exactly how big the blockchain was.

Fluffypony said the untouched blockchain was roughly two-and-a-half gigabytes but as soon as it got on a disk and became denormalized for its specific function, it would increase to a size around 10 gigabytes; obviously, it would continue increasing with time, although not at an abnormal rate like that found in Ethereum.

The correspondent asked how close the developers were to releasing the official GUI binaries for the Windows, Linux and Mac operating systems. He asked if fluffypony could enlighten him on the build's setup.

Fluffypony said that when Monero 0.10.1, which had been named "Wolfram Warptangent," is released, the team would publish as a distinct download the GUI binaries for all the prominent operating systems. The team was still waiting for programmers to round off some coding. He could foresee the team rolling out the new release at the end of the year. He also said the team's build set-up is composed of three versions of Mac, ARM, FreeBSD and many versions of Windows and Linux on 32-bit and 64-bit models.

In conclusion, the interviewer asked how fluffypony envisioned the future of digital currencies in general. He asked if the developer believed that enthusiasts would be taught cryptography in even the most basic courses in schools, creating a situation in which students could run their personal digital currency nodes in their own homes.

Fluffypony laughed, then said that in an ideal world, this could be possible. Humans are generally slow to change, although when they do eventually change, humans tend to adopt the change with all their hearts. He said it had been only a few years before then when everyone wanted to purchase a Blackberry device because it had a full keyboard, making every other phone almost useless. He added that in the present era, it was strange to picture or even imagine a physical keyboard on a phone.

Fluffypony said that as soon as users begin using cryptocurrencies for transactions and not investments, everyone will see the creation of an economy in which all or most transactions are conducted with similar patterns of payment. Fluffypony said that already such instances have begun to occur. He cited Backpage as an example. The website is merely for the exchange of goods and services. Fluffypony said that the site had removed payments through MasterCard and Visa; only the option of Bitcoin transactions remained.

This policy led to staff members being paid with Bitcoin. Staff was then encouraged to pay for their rent using Bitcoin. Fluffypony said that in the next seven to 10 years, the cyclic digital currency economy will have blended in so much that users will not need to constantly exchange their currencies into Euros or dollars. In the end, cryptocurrencies will have defeated such currencies. It is only a matter of time.

VERDICT

The year 2016 was one of outstanding achievements and progress for cryptocurrencies such as Bitcoin and Ethereum, as their values increased rapidly. However, Monero's progress that year outshone that of every other cryptocurrency. Monero's value multiplied so that it was worth about 27 times more than its value in 2015 (50 cents to $12). At one point, the rapid increment was at 2,760%, which quickly qualified it for the status of highest grossing digital currency for 2016. Currently, Monero's market value is about $165 million. Far from its decentralized mode of operations, the rapid growth of Monero boils down to its advanced privacy protocols. Not only are funds untraceable, but external authorities such as banks and governments have no control over Monero's activities. This is one reason why people seek to acquire digital currencies and Monero in particular.

Internet communities that wish to transact anonymously can already do so with the advent of Monero. Due to Monero's unprecedented acceptance, the Alphabay website published a public rally for the cryptocurrency in 2016. The site's administrators urged exchange platforms to integrate the digital currency into their systems.

In an interview, a prominent developer in the Monero platform; Spagni, said, *"That uptick among people who really need to be private is interesting."* He added, *"If it's good enough for a drug dealer, it is good enough for everyone else."*

CHAPTER 17: NEM (XEM)

Due to the growing interest in cryptocurrency in Japan, NEM quickly rose in popularity from the pool of other altcoins. Its token is XEM, which has also steadily increased in value since its launch. NEM is a digital currency written in Java. Its idea of worldwide distribution as well as important improvements on its native blockchain have given NEM a pass mark in Japan. An EigenTrust++ reputation, a proof-of-maintenance algorithm, encrypted messaging and multi-signature accounts are some of the improvements on its blockchain.

Due to these improvements, NEM's blockchain is already being used by many financial institutions in Japan as well as in countries around the world. Its blockchain is widely regarded as Mijin. NEM's team has been relentless in its bid to develop the cryptocurrency, a fact reflected in its constant updates and continued integration of many programs within its network.

Developer Makoto Takemiya is responsible for the creation and development of NEM. As an expert in the field, Takemiya's interest in digital currencies grew steadily. After working with some government and financial institutions, he decided to create a new currency, which became known as NEM.

THE ANNALS OF NEM

"NEM is a movement that aims to empower individuals by creating a new economy based on the principles of decentralization, financial freedom, and equality of opportunity." – NEM Technical Reference

NEM was intended to be a fork of Nxt but the interest in building an entirely new coin grew instead. This led a Bitcointalk participant, Utopian Future, to initiate a discussion about it on a Bitcointalk forum. Other participants were encouraged to join in the formal launch of NEM on the 19th of January 2014. Those who contributed to the project's development were promised 2.25 million XEM coins. However, the NEM project had not been legalized. The project continued regardless and those who had contributed to its development were given their stakes proportionally. Subsequently, all funds not claimed were diverted towards the development of NEM.

A beta version of the network was launched on the 20th of October 2014, after an initial launch, referred to as its alpha version. Its standard version was not launched until March 31, 2015. Already, there is a planned upgrade to another version which will be referred to as "Catapult."

A Japanese analyst named Koji Higashi commented on the continued popularity of NEM: *"NEM is popular thanks to the strong backing of the platform from the Zaif exchange, which is one of the biggest exchanges in Japan along with bitFlyer and coincheck. NEM's private blockchain solution developed by Zaif with NEM's core developers is called MIJIN and has established itself as a strong brand in the crypto space in Japan."*

However, he warned that users who did not have a concrete understanding of NEM's vision had begun to invest in it. He said this could be detrimental to NEM's future.

He added, *"Another thing to note about this new trend is that the general lack of understanding or appreciation of the technology by many of the new users. This is no surprise and all of us have been there at one point but the new wave of Japanese investors seems to be exhibiting a whole new level of incomprehension and misguided decision making in my opinion."*

Some notable developments that have taken place since its

launch include the release of the NEM Apostille, the emergence of NEM's technology-based financial projects, the release of Nano Wallets, and the transforming of NEM into a globally recognized platform. XEM's smallest unit is called microXEM.

THE ALPHA AND BETA VERSIONS

After a successful test of the program's alpha version, a much more complex version, the beta version, was introduced in October 2014. Although the NEM Foundation is represented publicly in Japan, all NEM developers are anonymous.

THE STRUCTURE OF NEM

NEM's structure includes two properties. The first property is regarded as the NEM infrastructure server or node while the second structure is used to manage the nodes. NEM also has a wallet named the Nano wallet. It is built with JavaScript and HTML codes. This makes it compatible with all Internet browsers. To send transaction details to the network, the embedded NIS program interacts with the Nano wallet.

Another program on NEM's network is the NEM community client. This was integrated into NEM's network with NIS and acts as a form of wallet within the system. However, Nano wallet's dominance has rendered it almost useless within the network. The firewall protection for Nano wallets helps protect it from hacks. NEM's network can be accessed on any computer, as it requires low computing power. Therefore, as soon as users connect to NIS, they can access NEM's network.

FEATURES

NAMESPACES: Namespaces is a naming program similar to the ICANN domain naming program. The program contains different levels of domains and subdomains. Therefore, users are allowed to create many subdomains for different accounts in the network.

REPUTATION OF NODES: The actions of all nodes within NEM's network are monitored by the EigenTrust++ program. This program monitors and ensures qualitative interactions and actions in NEM's network. Because quality of work is a prominent aspect of the network, efficiency is guaranteed on most occasions.

PROOF OF IMPORTANCE ALGORITHM: The number of transactions a user makes and the amount of NEM the user has determines the user's importance within the platform. A proof-of-importance algorithm validates or timestamps transactions within the network. Compared to other schemes that thrive on transaction fees, NEM's transactions consider quantity and trust to be important factors. This way, users are forced to constantly transact with their XEM coins instead of retaining them in their wallets.

HARVESTING: Harvesting is the process of creating a block. A synchronized and booted node as well as a minimum of 10,000 XEM are required to harvest any block.

SUPERNODES: The NEM Foundation rewards users who continuously transact within the platform through the supernodes program. Supernodes also help users directly connect to NEM's blockchain.

MESSAGING: Encrypted and unencrypted messages can be sent from one address to another during transactions in the NEM network. While the fee for sending unencrypted messages is 1 XEM, the fees for sending encrypted messages are not constant.

MULTISIGNATURE TRANSACTIONS: Multisignature is another program in NEM's network. It is a feature which ensures that all signatories validate a transaction before it is confirmed. In other words, an account within the platform can be owned by many users whose collective approval is required before transactions in such accounts can be shared on the network. NEM's developers have specified that the Catapult, a new version, will have advanced uses for the multisignature program.

MIJIN: Mijin is a mini blockchain within NEM's platform which seeks to make banking more secure. Some Japanese banks have already used it since its launch in December 2015. Within its chain, an uncountable number of assets is supported. Even though it is still being developed, it promises to be anther outstanding blockchain from NEM's developers.

FOOD FOR THOUGHT

Muhammad Yafi, a coordinator at the NEM Association of Malaysia and foundation, reconstructed an interview with Jeff McDonald, which was originally conducted by a Reddit user, "harshpokharna." The piece reads as follows:

QUESTION: "Do you think NEM is striving to be more successful than Bitcoin? Or can one say it is much better than the Bitcoin?"

RESPONSE: "Looking at some aspects, I can tell you that it is true. For instance, NEM is actually in multiple folds, effective and accurate in providing security for its platform if the upkeep cost is the yardstick being used. That fundamentally implies that those who mine Bitcoin are constantly wasting about a million dollars or more of Bitcoin every day so as to ensure that Bitcoin continues to exist but all of the harvesters in NEM rarely have to incur any expense whatsoever. The question now is what is the relevance of that situation? I think I should explain it from the opposite angle. What will NEM have as its market cap if one million US dollars constantly comes in every day? I think we can both agree that it will be much higher than Bitcoin's market cap in the long run.

"Along with the upcoming important launch, we also have plans to create a main net which would scale in Tx/S more than ten folds when compared to Bitcoin. In addition, when it comes to the features too, I can say that NEM has an advantage that can be said to more than ten times when compared as well. Try to picture that "CounterParty" has been integrated into Bitcoin's network. That can be likened to NEM Mosaics but the Mosaics are on a higher level.

"Also picture Namecoin being included in Bitcoin's platform. That can be likened to Namespaces as well. Yet, Namespaces are marginally better.

"Furthermore, try to picture that messages are being permitted to be integrated directly into Bitcoin's network in an appropriate way and not in a way through which people would begin to hack into the OP Return. Envision a comprehensive multisig software just like Bitpay's Copay being integrated into NEM's network. With that as well, NEM's provision is still more superior. It is not just in words, it is what it is.

"NEM's platform also has a spam protection feature, a thing Bitcoin has long yearned for. There is equally a good reputation for out nodes.

"Try to picture Factom that did not have a use for its own currency and also did not have to use its own network. In place of merely providing a plain, one-off timestamp or providing a timestamp transferable to other stakeholders, an upgradeable timestamp was provided that was capable of holding more memos. Presently, there is NEM's Apostille. Which is readily available for anyone as soon as they log into the NEM network."

QUESTION: "So you believe that your explanation is very adequate for revealing the reasons why NEM is ten times better than the Bitcoin. However, what can you say about Ethereum on the other hand?"

RESPONSE: "Actually, to a large extent, Ethereum is not scalable. I don't think it can scale. Therefore, I believe it will ultimately find itself in the same problem like Bitcoin as soon as users begin to constantly use it. NEM however, has been created from the onset to be scalable. Another thing is that Ethereum cannot be easily built on, neither is it very safe. In the NEM platform, third-party developers are given very easy APIs to create from and they are always a hundred percent safe. A question to be asked is where is Ethereum's Apostille or Ethereum's namespaces? There are some reasons for not being able to really find them. These two programs are actually in the Ethereum platform but they need some complex programming to build, even though these sorts of programming are easy to implement in NEM. That is why in some situations, NEM is by far easier to build and improve on than Ethereum regarding some particular types of software. However, in other scenarios, it might not be completely true.

"In some situations, the Ethereum platform can achieve some tasks which NEM can't and that is simply because the two networks are not the same.

"This means that even though a strong opinion can be formed based on the fact that NEM is permanently ten times better than Bitcoin, it is quite difficult to totally agree that the same advantage occurs when compared to Ethereum. However, in all, I think NEM's platform still has an advantage over that of Ethereum. One can see Ethereum as a platform in which one can do whatever he or she wants but with a little bit of accompanied difficulty. One the other hand, one can see NEM as a platform in which one can do so many important things with a relative ease. There is a way to go about each approach but none of the two is perfect."

QUESTION: "You mentioned that NEM comes with a spam protection feature. Is it realistic that users would make spam transactions to some other personal accounts which they hold so as to game the system?"

RESPONSE: "It is not likely. The NEM developers carried out a standard job of creating a comprehensive spam system that has many aspects of the formula. So, in the first place, if anyone makes different accounts and spams himself or herself, the miners or the harvesters will play along. They will accept the fees but the issue is if the user fills up all the available blocks so as to validate other transactions. In other words, users can spam, in as much as they are willing to pay for it. It only makes the harvesters happy. However, in a case where a user begins to tamper with other users' transactions, the situation is slightly different. Those accounts conducting multiple transactions would experience an increase in their fees while other stable and regular accounts like the one I have for instance would not experience the same. Almost immediately, the hacker would learn that transferring XEM from a particular account to a few others within a short time has increased his transaction fees significantly.

"This means that if the hacker is actually determined and creates five thousand accounts which he begins to use in bits and ultimately creates a network spam, he will realize that it is difficult to raise the transaction fees because it wouldn't just be one or a few number of accounts that would be flagged for creating spam. The system would then switch over to the Proof of importance algorithm (POI), which is NEM's consensus scheme in contradiction to Proof of work and Proof of stake algorithms that are found in some other blockchains."

He said that to effectively carry out a spam attack on any user's transaction by trying to censor the user, the perpetrator must have purchased so many units of XEM and then distributed them equally throughout the accounts. The attacker would then have to key them in for long periods through multiple accounts to ensure that such accounts had proofs of importance higher than those accounts about to be hacked.

He said it is possible that the attacker could then begin to spam the system by keeping the transactions of his targets within a single block. However, the NEM platform has taken the censorship structure to a whole new level. The users could raise their fees, which would require the attacker to increase his fees as well. This implies that if an attacker was to put a 100,000 XEM over 1,000 accounts, he would have to buy 100 million XEM, which is currently worth about two million dollars. That is one risk no one would be willing take. Should anyone try, Muhammad clearly said they could go ahead and do so.

In that case, the hacker would spend more than one million dollars, then have to wait patiently for weeks. He would spend more and more in transaction fees to successfully attack a platform, which would ultimately cause the market capitalization to drop significantly. This simply means the hacker would be able to sell only at a huge loss when he finally did try to exit.

In simple terms, there might never be a huge spam attack. NEM should be compared to Bitcoin, in which a user from the previous year could spend $5,000 to $6,000 within a day and get all the blocks equally filled and stop normal transactions afterwards. He said that NEM is 10 times a better option, considering the spam situation. He added that such precautions were not only applicable to the issue of spam but have been successfully blended with all of the issues the NEM developers have fixed.

He said that the soon-to-be launched version, Catapault, would serve as the single blockchain and the first of its kind, from which many organizations could benefit.

The question of how developers tackle spam was not correctly structured because it paints a picture of the network as lacking strength and requiring shielding from spam. In the true sense, the system only needs more transactions. He reiterated that the harvesters would only receive an opportunity to earn more coins. Even though the system wants only legitimate transactions, he said that a situation in which someone tried to stop another user's transaction would cost the person a huge amount of money—perhaps millions of dollars. It would also require a lengthy duration of time for planning and executing.

QUESTION: "This means you need more people to use NEM. Do you think that would not that affect decentralization just like Bitcoin? Can you say that NEM is more decentralized than Bitcoin?"

RESPONSE: "In the platform, we need transactions. However, in Bitcoin, administrators don't really want too many transactions due to the fact that there would be extensions in block sizes, which otherwise implies that there would be less full nodes. Don't forget that in Bitcoin, full nodes do not get rewarded. Miners are just running them for the sake of running only. Bitcoin has an altruistic structure that simply means that it cannot be scalable to be blunt.

"On the other hand, NEM users who run full nodes are getting rewarded. They are the platform's harvesters. Mining and launching a full node is synched in NEM and not put separately like it is in the Proof of work algorithm. That is Bitcoin's blockchain consensus scheme. In Proof of work, miners do not really care about other things apart from the rewards. Also, full node operators don't eventually get any reward. In NEM, all full node runners get rewarded and really care about the system as well since they are also direct stakeholders in the platform. The greater the rate at which transactions are being conducted, the better it is for harvesters. That implies that there would be more money to earn.

"I must also admit that NEM's block sizes would still later increase, which would make harvesters' hard drives get filled up quickly. However, they can easily afford many more hard drives with the huge rewards that they earn. It'll be great to have full blocks in NEM's network."

Muhammad said that in Bitcoin, the larger blocks cause centralization because a few users run a few nodes. There are also advancements in hardware in the proof-of-work algorithm, which implies that the mining process has gradually become a centralized process as well. Meanwhile, in NEM, the larger the blocks, the more decentralization increases. That is because some very light computers, for instance, a Pi 3 Raspberry, can be used to harvest in NEM. Currently, a user with a balance of 15,000 XEM plus a somewhat low proof-of-importance gauge may not be able to harvest. The reason for this is that the fees from creating blocks are not sufficient. However, if the block were completely filled, a harvester can turn on the Pi and produce some blocks in a month. Once these full blocks earn the user a total of five dollars or even more, many other users will likely begin to run the full nodes from their homes.

He also said that sometimes little investments can turn into rewards from harvesting. This process is quite easy; beginners can harvest as long as they follow instructions from the tutorial that has been made available. There are plans to make this procedure even easier in the future. Many people have no experience with mining before, due to its convenience and ease, they eventually try it with NEM. These participants and enthusiasts have learned that they can become an important part of the platform and earn some rewards. Harvesting nodes continue to increase as the platform enjoys decentralization. He ended by saying that when NEM's prospects are examined, a strong probability exists that it will become more decentralized as it grows.

QUESTION: "Let's say that there is a one-click mobile form of payment available in all prominent nations, can you already envision that people will adopt cryptocurrencies for their daily payments?"

RESPONSE: "It might be difficult to ascertain because many factors are at stake, which might ultimately cause a problem before this can happen. However, personally, I believe that there is a possibility, precisely in some of the markets that are not fervent or underrated."

CHAPTER 18: DIGITAL NOTE (XDN)

The DigitalNote cryptocurrency is an open-source currency with a decentralized and secure blockchain structure. Transactions and exchanges are instantly encrypted, with no leaks through which they can be traced. The coins are mined through a very secure CPU mining procedure which is largely resistant to ASIC. It also features a blockchain platform which pays interest on deposits. The network's coin is represented as XDN. DigitalNote was formerly known as Darknote.

The platform was built using the anonymously designed technology known as CryptoNote. However, it has some additional features, such as encrypted messages. The platform has no central administrator, as it uses a peer-to-peer structure. Its mining scheme is also an advanced proof of work (POW) process not monitored by anyone within the platform.

Its network ensures automatic and secure exchanges and transactions with the hidden transfer of messages. Charges for transactions on the platform are relatively low. XDN is secured using complex mathematical calculations, which ultimately help individuals manage their personal financial progress as well as monitor information that is being shared. Users' private keys are equivalent to banks accounts, although in this case no one censors or surveys the user accounts.

FEATURES

The maximum number of XDN that will ever be mined and be kept in circulation is 8,589,869,056. The reward for each block produced is about 150 XDN. DigitalNote is a distinct version of the financial economy that uses blockchain technology. The mining procedure is predictable because miners earn a constant reward whenever a new block is created.

Furthermore, DigitalNote remains the only digital currency with blockchain deposits whose interest rate, on a yearly basis, is between 0.4 to 1.09 percent. Also, the block target time is around four minutes, which makes the transaction process almost three times faster than that of Bitcoin. Another amazing feature is that the mining procedure is so easy it can be performed on an average computer system.

DigitalNote's platform also makes micropayments easy. The transaction fee starts at only 0.001XDN.

WALLETS

A typical user can use DigitalNote's graphic wallet. The "Simple Wallet" program stores services such as coin exchanges and mining pools. Binary files can also be downloaded, and users can simply organize their personal XDN verified stores.

Some wallets that are built specifically for services include the DigitalNote wallet for Linux, the DigitalNote wallet for Windows (32 and 64 bit), the DigitalNote wallet for OSx and a few others.

It has similar provisions for personal use as well.

ACQUIRING XDN

Users can acquire DigitalNote through mining. Because the mining process creates new sets of the cryptocurrency, miners receive these new units as a reward for ensuring the security of DigitalNote's network through their CPU power.

Another medium through which to acquire XDN is deposits. All XDN users can make XDN deposits, which offer an annual interest rate of about one percent. Users can also lock their XDN for periods ranging from one month to 10 years. In addition, XDN can be exchanged for other forms of cryptocurrency, and users can opt to receive payment for transactions or services through XDN.

The platform also has some notable mining pools, such as "Start your pool," "Waiting post HF pools," minergrate.com, DigitalNoteTalk and blockchain explorer.

EXCHANGE PLATFORMS

Exchange platforms into which DigitalNote has already been integrated include the Bittrex exchange, the HitBTC exchange and many others.

Subsequent developments in the platform will include a proof-of-activity scheme built on the mobile client, digital identification for blockchain, nicknames for messages and blockchain deposits.

CHAPTER 19: YBCOIN

YBCoin is also known as Yua Bao Coin and is a digital currency that originated in China. Like other newly introduced digital currencies, it was created by a set of technology geeks who admired Bitcoin's network and protocol. These geeks decided to produce a considerate, open-source and transparent cryptocurrency which could be easily accessed. They focused on eliminating the prominent flaws in Bitcoin's network.

In China, Yua Bao represents a process of evaluating silver and gold. Therefore, the platform is named Yua Bao because the creators want the platform to be considered a community in which unlimited fortunes and riches can be acquired if sensible investments are made.

Currently, its platform is built on a source code structure in which all transactions are conducted through a peer-to-peer communication procedure. It already has more than 100,000 participants, which automatically make it an elite cryptocurrency in China. More users continue to sign up for the platform. At this rate, YBCoin is set to overtake standard cryptocurrencies that have been in existence before it entered the mainstream platforms. Its market capitalization has already reached three million dollars. YBCoin also has a strong and reliable structure which has fostered its constant growth. The cryptocurrency can be said to have a promising future.

Its developers have begun making plans to spread the coin beyond China. However, most of its features and functions have yet to be translated into English, which has hindered the platform's development. In addition, YBCoin's block time is around 60 seconds, which has not helped with respect to the cryptocurrency's expected development rate. There have been calls for a greatly reduced block time.

YBCoin offers a somewhat economical version, which has been drastically realigned to match network power that balances incentives for mining.

MINING PROCESS

YBCoin uses complex proof-of-stake and proof-of-work mining algorithms that effectively monitor inflation rates and prevent the loss of capital. Therefore, YBCoin guarantees stability and progress for members who have invested in the network. Many cryptocurrency market forums have expressed their respect for this approach. At the moment, about three million coins are being circulated. Additional coins have yet to be minted, although there is a yearly proof-of-stake interest, which is about one percent. The platform already has more than 100,000 participants, and the possibility is strong that this number will keep increasing due to the platform's constant development. In addition to its positive reputation and supportive community, YBCoin offers important functions that can be used to shape major digital currency markets in the near future.

FEATURES

YBCoin employs a hybrid scheme including the scrypt-based proof-of-work and proof-of-stake procedures. The digital currency is also a fork of YACoin. It uses a hash algorithm that can be represented as "Chacha 20 / 8 + scrpyt." The time for block targets within the platform is equivalent to one minute. In addition, the highest proof-of-work rewards or earnings are 10 coins.

YBCoin's certified website is http://www.ybcoin.org/

PROCESS OF DEVELOPMENT

YBCoin's developers typically conduct operations within their personal trees. They put forward pull requests once they believe their solutions to bugs or developmental programs have been effective.

These patches are immediately welcomed and participants reach a general consensus. Developers are also encouraged to tweak some provided fixes should they not work with the platform's coding protocols or be assumed to present some controversies.

A head branch is constantly developed and tested. However, there is no assurance that it is stable and reliable. Usually, tags are produced to point out newly developed, reliable and stable versions of the platform. Some branches are also developed if many developers are creating an important program.

Over time, pull requests usually run out of usability. That is, they become outdated. Once this occurs, such pulls would instantly not be possible to merge. Still, there are usually comments on the pulls, which serve as warnings about their closure. Fifteen days after the broadcast of a warning, the pulls will be closed if their producers have done nothing to regulate them. Any pull closed in such a manner will be tagged as "stagnant."

Other issues, like "no commits," are addressed through similar warning notes. They are also closed after 15 days if nothing is done to rectify them. The 15-day countdown begins from their last active time and such issues are tagged as "stale."

CHAPTER 20: UNDERSTANDING BLOCKCHAIN TECHNOLOGY

While a compound word (block-chain) comes to the mind whenever the word "blockchain" is seen or said, the conventional meanings of these two words do not represent the term's definition.

BLOCKCHAIN TECHNOLOGY

The invention of blockchain technology was a noble breakthrough in the ICT world. Although it is unclear whether the creator was a single individual or a group of computer geeks, blockchain is widely known to be a masterpiece of Satoshi Nakamoto. Since its introduction, it has transformed–and continues to transform–into a program that everyone is trying to take advantage of.

Blockchain technology has successfully introduced an integral aspect of the modern-day internet through the seamless but uncopyable distribution of digital information. It is said to have been initially developed for Bitcoin (the first digital money) but geeks around the world have found new and even better ways to manipulate the technology as well.

Candidly, an average enthusiast doesn't need to know the technicalities of blockchain technology before he or she can use it. However, curiosity about why it has created so much buzz has forced many to learn how it works.

Blockchain serves as virtual storage for all types of transactions. It is wired in a way to allow for the compilation and storage of diverse digital monetary transactions as well as other valuables.

Essentially, the mechanism of a blockchain can be likened to an accounting catalogue that has been copied so many times on some computer's network that it is being updated periodically through the network.

KEY FEATURES

INFORMATION IS PUBLIC

All pieces of information on a blockchain are regarded as "shared." Its database is public and very much accessible because it is not caged down in a particular location on the web. Its data is actively and simultaneously processed by largely uncountable computers. Hence, there is no centralized information that could be destabilized. Simply put, everyone on the network can easily obtain access to the data of a blockchain.

Another example that vividly explains the operations within a blockchain is as follows: A piece of writing due to be published must go through the editing and proofreading process before it is tagged as ready for public consumption. This means the piece will pass through different specialists who will in turn work independently and continue to pass along the piece until it eventually gets to the publisher. The process of passing the piece of writing from one expert to another could distort the information's initial importance. Therefore, a setback could occur. One can only imagine the gravity of such distortions if they affect legal documents.

Although blockchain technology was not invented for the analogy above, certain economic activities followed such patterns before the massive turn towards the blockchain.

Indeed, passing around documents and information in a non-secure manner is a risk that has been successfully managed by blockchain technology. Not only does it allow different stakeholders to access the same piece of information simultaneously without any form of disruption, it also ensures the free flow of data.

Just as the Internet has done for the approximately 30 years since its inception, a blockchain stores many blocks of information that are similar to its network. This makes it impossible for a single user to have absolute control. In addition, blockchain technology has not had any instances of failure. In fact, since the launch of the first digital currency (Bitcoin) in 2008, its blockchain has operated without any major disruptions. The traceable shortcomings are the result of humans who transacted within the blockchain. It continues to be reliable as the years pass, and it is encouraging that from time to time improvements are made in terms of its maintenance.

Recently, an expert, Ian Khan, said that blockchain has begun to foster accountability and perfection in the finance world. This means that transaction errors, be they the result of humans or machines, will gradually minimize should blockchain technology take over the sector completely.

For almost 30 years, the internet has proven itself to be a durable phenomenon. Its track record bodes well for blockchain technology as it is developed. Khan also said that a blockchain ensures that financial transactions are valid. This is because the technology, through a secure process, helps duplicate a register on many other connected systems of registers.

LIMPID AND IMPENETRABLE

Blockchain is designed to automatically run a check once every 10 minutes. This is consistently carried out without any record of glitches. Widely referred to as a "completed block", this routine check serves as a form of digital auditing as the network processes every activity that occurs within it during those 10-minute intervals. A block can be defined as an integral part of a blockchain that is responsible for recording recent information or transactions. Once the recording is complete, the data ports into the database and therefore becomes a permanent part of it. Upon the completion of a certain block, another is instantly formed. These blocks continue to grow due to the addition of completed "blocks" to the blockchain's database. Already, the system contains many blocks and the number keeps increasing. However, the blocks are properly linked to one another according to their time of completion, i.e., chronologically. Every block has the hash of the previous block within it.

All data on the blockchain has been credibly made public. More importantly, it is largely incorruptible. Except in cases in which the entire network is overridden, information on the blockchain cannot be altered. Even the supposed override isn't practicable in that sense. Hacking into the blockchain system to cart bitcoins or any other cryptocurrency would instantly destroy their value, rendering such attempts futile.

Don Tapscott is one of the most reputable enthusiasts in the world when it comes to blockchain technology, advanced media, revolutionary innovation, and the economic and societal influence of these modern-day technologies.

An in-depth interview he conducted with blockchain expert Gary Nuttall reads as follows:

Tapscott asked, "What gave you the inspiration to produce 'Blockchain Revolution?'"

Nuttall responded that three years before then, he had a discussion with his son, Alex, during a father-and-son ski trip. He was an executive at an investment bank and had also taken responsibility for their growing deal flow for Bitcoin startups. He said that he was writing the introduction to the 20th-anniversary edition of *The Digital Economy* and was also looking into cryptocurrencies as the next big thing in technology. One thing led to the next and he decided to engage in several research projects exploring how blockchain might change business and the world.

Tapscott next asked why people needed to pay attention to blockchain technology. Nuttall's answer was that the technology is nothing less than the Internet's second era. He said that for decades the Internet of information had been in existence. Currently, the world had the Internet of value, which would create profound changes in the nature of firms: how they are funded and managed, how they create value, and how they perform basic functions like marketing, accounting, manufacturing and innovation. In some cases, software will replace management altogether.

Nuttall said that blockchain technology can help fix the deep structures and architecture of the government and the creation of public value. He added that a second era of democracy could ultimately be built based on accountability to citizens, transparency and a culture of public deliberation. In a broad way, technology has given those individuals who want a better world another kick at the can in terms of rewriting the economic power grid and the old order.

Tapscott asked Nuttall how blockchain technology would rebrand the financial services industry. Nuttall provided an example. He said that he agreed with Ben Lawsky, former superintendent of financial services for New York State, who had mentioned that in five to 10 years, the industry would probably be unrecognizable. Whether it would be the incumbents or the new players who did the disrupting remained to be seen. He mentioned a statement he had brought up earlier in regards to the paradigm shift in 1993, in which the leaders of old paradigms typically had great difficulty embracing a new one.

Nuttall said that the best short (18-minute) overview of how blockchains will rebrand this industry was Alex Tapscott's TEDX San Francisco talk, titled, "Blockchain is Eating Wall Street." He said that an interview by Richtopia documented it.

Essentially, a blockchain's most significant characteristic is that it allows the disruption of any business model that may necessitate an intermediate body. The insurance value chain has various bodies in between, each of which believes it is providing value instead of increasing costs.

Nuttall said that his work in the London Commercial Insurance Market was creating new means of visualizing the value chain amongst clients with a capital benefactor. Thus, the risk is significantly reduced.

In addition, he said, "Brokers talk about removing the need for Underwriters and Underwriters question the need for Brokers in a future model. Blockchain enables both approaches and we could see radical changes in operating models as well as new products and services being developed. It's possible that insurance may be augmented (or replaced) by alternative financial instruments that can be developed using blockchain. As an example, think of an insurance contract sliced into individual components that can then be traded in a marketplace—a new derivatives marketplace. Other financial sectors have Swaps or Options, and they could extend to insurance as alternative mechanisms for risk mitigation."

NODES AND BLOCKCHAIN

Blockchain technology is also made up of "computing nodes." Nodes are tasked with validating transactions. They instantly download copies of a blockchain as soon as they join the blockchain network. Nodes and blockchain produce a very strong network which ultimately refines the internet's functionality.

On the blockchain, each node functions as an administrator. A node freely joins the network, thereby decentralizing it. However, there is a reward for participation–the earning of a cryptocurrency such as Bitcoin. Generally, nodes are believed to be mining cryptocurrencies but that is a mischaracterization. Rather, each node struggles to win these digital currencies by finding solutions to computer-based puzzles.

DECENTRALIZATION

Another milestone to note in the appraisal of blockchain technology is the idea of decentralization. The entire network is actively involved with the smallest of activities on it, which indicates that all transactions are verified on the blockchain simultaneously and are readily visible to all connected users. Unlike the conventional commercial process, the stock market (for instance, decentralization and transparency) is already embedded in the conduct of blockchain transactions.

Furthermore, decentralization is practiced on a blockchain network through a peer-to-peer operation within it, which allows for a considerable amount of collaboration.

UNCRACKABLE SECURITY

Blockchain technology is indeed a breakthrough in the tech world but its formidability and continued reliability boils down to the decentralization of data within its network. Data is spread across all parts of the network, making it essentially impossible for hackers to infiltrate. Before now, the system of securing online accounts through passwords had many loopholes but the encryption mechanism in blockchain technology has effectively halted any sort of hacking. Through a randomly generated string of keys, users can secure their accounts on the blockchain network. These keys are widely known as "public keys." They are essentially users' personal addresses within the blockchain. All transactions are typically traced to each user's address within the network. Another form of advanced encryption that has always been in operation in the blockchain is the use of "private keys." These keys are similar to passwords, which give all users access to their digital money. However, it is expedient for every user to create a paper wallet to protect their "private key."

THE BLOCKCHAIN DOMINANCE

The web has had a rebranded function since the introduction of blockchain technology. What is generally known as the peer-to-peer form of transaction is already very productive in today's world. Users on the platform can easily conduct transactions with one another directly. According to records, an average of 200,000 dollars in Bitcoin transactions was conducted daily in 2016. Barring any future challenges, one can say that the security of blockchain transactions will ultimately change modes of operation, even within native financial institutions.

An associate professor at Brown University in Berkeley, George Howard, said that the year 2017 would be a very important one with respect to the prospects and future of the technology behind the blockchain structure. He said that the organizations using it would likely start raising money by creating products or services that the market demands or values.

George Howard also said that 2017 would be a year in which the number of products employing blockchain technology would increase significantly. There would not be many discussions about the technology being "magical pixie dust" that could be spread everywhere. He said that the publicity would not only come from users but also from across sectors, and everyone would want to have an experience with it. The technology would be somewhat hidden even though its functions and structure would continue to help private and commercial users solve their immediate and long-term problems.

George also said that he was personally conversant with several large-scale blockchain technology use cases that would be launching sometime in 2017. More importantly, he said that the implementation stage which 2017 represented would be a vital step in the larger adoption of the blockchain because it would allow skeptics to see the functionality instead of just hearing about its promise.

USABILITY OF BLOCKCHAIN TECHNLOGY

As mentioned earlier, one doesn't need to understand the intricacies of the blockchain before putting it to good use. However, in recent times the finance sector has arguably been indebted to the invention of the technology, as it has dominantly flocked activities within it. An estimated sum of 430 billion USD was transferred two years ago using the blockchain. Currently, there is a significant scramble for blockchain programmers.

Blockchain technology principally eliminates third parties in financial transactions. The introduction of GUI (Graphic User Interface) has transformed personal computing into publicly accessible computing. "Wallets" are some of the most popular GUIs designed for the blockchain. Over the years, users have been able to buy things on these platforms through the use of cryptocurrencies. However, transactions have been successful partly because of the validation of identity processes. Wallet applications will certainly become more efficient in the future with the introduction of more methods through which to manage users' identities.

ORGANIZATIONS THAT HAVE ALREADY TAPPED INTO THE RESOURCES OF BOCKCHAIN TECHNOLOGY

While many are still skeptical about the technology's reliability, notable companies have begun to maximize its potential. Some of these companies are: ANZ, ASX, Enome.io, BLOCKCHAIN Australia, Post Capgemini, CoinJar, IBM, Data61 and Commonwealth Bank.

THE PLAUSIBLE RELEVANCE OF THE BLOCKCHAIN

In the blockchain network, users can authenticate digital information, creating value in the process. In the business world, this form of accessibility has basic implications, as seen in:

1) **SMART CONTRACTS:** Because ledgers are distributed, the encoding of simple contracts is enabled so that they will execute when certain conditions are met.

2) **CROWDFUNDING:** Sites like GoFundMe and Kickstarter have been piloting the peer form of transactions. Their popularity indicates that internet users want to be directly involved in product development. Blockchain technology has taken this desire to a higher level through the creation of new crowd-sourced funds. One example of this is the creation of The DAO (decentralized autonomous organization) in 2016. The DAO raised around $200 million in about two months. Those who participated could vote on smart contract capital investments after they had purchased "DAO Tokens." However, there were dire consequences when some project funds were hacked. It was later discovered that this particular project had been initiated without an appropriate or detailed structuring. In all, the birth of The DAO implies that the blockchain can foster a renewed form of economic agreement.

3) **COMPREHENSIVE AUDITING:** There's already an increment in the rate at which customers strive to ascertain whether all the claims a company makes about its products are genuine. Distributed ledgers have provided an easy means of verifying that the things customers have read about a product are real, even before the purchase. Prompt stamping of the location and time of production on a product fosters transparency within the network. For instance, the Ethereum blockchain has an origin pilot project which ensures that goods sold at specific locations have been adequately supplied by the actual suppliers from their specified regions.

4) **ADMINISTRATIVE EASE:** The distributed database technology that operates within the blockchain network makes results transparent and accessible to the public should it be employed in an election or other types of polls. For instance, smart contracts would assist in automating the entire process without glitches. Smooth decision-making processes are achieved using the Boardroom application on the blockchain. Therefore, the process of managing digital monies or assets becomes instantly transparent, accessible and reliable. Equity is encouraged in the process.

5) **STORAGE:** The distribution of data throughout the blockchain network enables the protection of important files. This decentralized process of file storage on the net offers a significant advantage, as it does not permit data loss.

The IPFS (inter-planetary file system) encourages the formation of operations in a distributed web. The IPFS completely eliminates the need for client-server relationships, which will speed up file transfers and other transactions on the net. This form of processing is not just ideal but also a mandatory improvement on the web's overloaded content-delivery systems.

6) **PERFECT PREDICTIONS:** The Augur application on the blockchain creates essential offerings with respect to the outcome of real events. For instance, by placing stakes on correct predictions regarding shares, participants can easily earn money. Payouts will subsequently increase according to the correct outcome of shares purchased. Blockchain is a technology that thrives on the crowd's recommendation. Hence, the indication is strong that in the future other, similar applications will be developed on the network.

7) **SECURE PROTECTION OF PROPERTIES:** Smart contracts on the blockchain can adequately automate the trade of creative materials online, effectively erasing the risks of file redistribution or copying. Before now, copyright owners had been on the receiving end because digital information can be replicated without limits, thereby giving internet users a mountain of free content. However, the deployment of smart contracts will ensure that the unjust lifting of intellectual property is kept to a minimum.

8) **THE IDEOLOGY OF IOT:** IoT is a form of management typically controlled on a network. Because smart contracts are responsible for the automated management of remote systems, IOT applications on the blockchain will process everything from the maintenance of mechanical aspects to the analysis of data and automated management. This yields efficiency and adequate monitoring. Today, some big names in the telecommunications sector are advocating the consistent use of IoT applications. This is because an automated run of their remote devices will help with their maintenance.

9) **CONTROL OF IDENTITY:** The need to manage users' identities cannot be overemphasized. Identity verification is a source of credibility in online transactions. However, risks related to security have caused worry among participants. Distributed ledgers, as found on the blockchain, have advanced the

methods of proving one's identity; this includes the provision of digitalized personal bio-data and documents. This management of identity ultimately brands users as having good reputations, thereby promoting additional transactions in the future. Regardless of the processes said above, the improvement of identity standards in the digital world has been a tedious process. A plausible and reliable identification process requires unification of the government and private sectors. Currently, electronic commerce on the net depends on the SSL certificate for safe transactions. Netki is a startup application that seeks to create an SSL standard for the blockchain.

10) **PROTECTION AGAINST FRAUD:** Until now, financial institutions have had to complete rigorous processes for every one of their new customers to certify their intentions and identities. These hectic processes, commonly known as AML (anti-money laundering) and KYC (know your customer) policies, can and will eventually be practiced within the blockchain network. For instance, the startup Polycoin provides a solution similar to AML and KYC in transaction analysis. It forwards all suspicious transactions to compliance officers. The cost of KYC, therefore, will be significantly reduced due to the verification process within the blockchain. TiM (trust in motion) is another picture-based application, on the Tradle startup. It helps users upload a screenshot of important files; as soon as financial institutions verify the files, the blockchain stores the data cryptographically.

11) **REGISTRATION OF PROPERTIES:** The blockchain can enhance all forms of record keeping due to its publicly accessible ledgers. Many countries around the world have begun administering blockchain-based registry projects, primarily on landed properties, as these titles are prone to fraud and other negative situations. Although the project's current situation is not very clear, Honduras became the first country to embark on

such reforms in 2015. Georgia also agreed on a deal with a tech group to invent a blockchain technology for property titles in the country.

12) **TRADING OF STOCKS:** A countless number of stock and commodity exchanges are already using the blockchain methodology in the various services they provide. This is because it has been discovered that, with the blockchain, peer-to-peer transactions are carried out instantly and adequately without the assistance or involvement of traditional intermediaries in the stock market. Furthermore, the use of blockchain technology means that stock trading would not need the well-known auditors or custodians. Not long ago, an announcement was made about the introduction of a blockchain project on the Estonian Stock Market.

13) **PUBLISHING:** Mass media has not been left out. An article on Credit Suisse said that one could argue that media houses and publications can reap gains from the initiation of a blockchain-based payment system known as Micro Payments. This type of payment can be introduced for articles and informative content publicized within a blockchain platform. The article also said that micropayments could serve as a diverse means of integrating a new payment structure, notwithstanding the existing subscription charges made on a monthly or yearly basis. The writer warned that no concrete proof yet existed that participants would uniformly accept such developments, as they must be certain about any payment they made within the platform.

The writer also specified that it is not certain that blockchain technology could carry out tasks to change the progression of qualitative adverts from their current forms to online platforms that would essentially operate on the blockchain.

In other words, blockchain technology will likely not influence the prospects of current internet-based private business forums. However, producers from the medical, technical and scientific fields could use the technology to initiate and complete financial transactions, organize their programs, receive payment from the government and academic institutions, and create an avenue for feedback from their readers. Still, a few computer programs currently address these needs effectively; we would expect that current tools are proficient in these functions.

The writer also pointed out that experts and researchers would likely not be able to disrupt the STM journal-publishing industry by using payments for private articles or books. It is well-known that publishers withdraw a tangible portion of economic value. The author also added that, to an extent, he believed blockchain technology would not overtake the existing economic structure because the brand-name, peer-studied journal is still required for quality, prestige, the gathering of funds and the acquisition of tenure by academics.

PROBABLE DOWNSIDE

As in every other sector, blockchain technology has disadvantages.

An objective analysis of some potential negative implications was documented by a technical report from the Sutardja Center for Entrepreneurship & Technology. Excerpts from the explicit analysis are as follows.

Blockchain technology is a breakthrough in the computing world with uncountable promises. There are already so many types of applications or difficulties whose solutions can be found with the assistance of a blockchain-related technology. This ranges from financial, i.e., remittance to investment banking, to non-financial cases such as notary services.

Many of the innovations are largely radical in nature and in cases where these sorts of innovations have been widely adopted, they always come with some specific associated risks

Scaling: The scaling of existing nascent programs based on the blockchain poses difficulties. Take the instance of the process of carrying out a transaction using the blockchain as a first time user. One would have to pass through downloading a total set of the currently active blockchains and verify before one's foremost transaction can be processed. That would take many hours or even days depending on the rate at which the number of blocks keep increasing exponentially.

Behavior Change: One thing is particularly constant in life and that is change. However, some situations don't yield to change. In an era in which there is a non-tangible trusted third party that the blockchain stands for, users have to become aware of the permanent fact that their electronic transactions are complete, safe and relatively secure. In the case of credit cards, the modern day intermediaries including third parties like MasterCard and Visa will also experience the switch of responsibility and roles. It has been envisioned such platforms would also make investments and shift their platforms to be blockchain-based ones. Thereafter, they will progress to provide services relating to customer relationship.

Fraudulent Activities: Due to the secretive nature of blockchain transactions, as well as the convenience it offers when moving valuables, those who are bent on perpetrating negative acts may take advantage of this secretive nature to engage in fraudulent acts like the trafficking of money. However, law enforcement agencies would be capable of watching and prosecuting them as long as there are technological supports and concrete regulation strategies.

Government Regulations: The adoption of blockchain

191

based transactions in the modern world may be slowed down by Government agencies such as the SEC and FTC among many others. This could be done through the introduction of new rules to control and preside over the activities within the sector so as to ensure that users comply strictly. This idea may help increase its acceptance in the US because such agencies already try to ensure that their customers trust them completely. However, the adoption of such regulations in some countries whose economies are more controlled, for instance, China, may have significant disadvantages.

Bootstrapping: The shift of business documents, frameworks and existing contracts to the new blockchain based methodology would pose a tasking procedure of migration activities which need to be carried out. For example, in a situation of Real Estate license and ownerships, the existing papers which lie in Escrow or County organizations that have to be migrated to the corresponding blockchain structure. This would be costly and time consuming.

Quantum Computing: The core idea of the blockchain technology is its reliability [in terms of] the convincing fact that it is not mathematically possible for just one user to exclusively gain access to the system due to [the] insufficient availability of the needed computing power. However, with the possible future production and disbursement of Quantum Computers, the cryptographic keys would certainly be very easy to break with the employment of [a] "sheer, brute, energy" strategy within a short period of time. This would ultimately make the whole system crumble emphatically. A way to prevent this form of disaster is to ensure that keys get stronger and become increasingly harder to crack or hack. (Source: Sutardja)

In conclusion, the blockchain is the powerhouse for all cryptocurrencies. Perhaps the future will see more responsibilities placed on the technology. However, for now, it remains the system that enables the remarkable activities of digital currency.

GLOSSARY

Alchemist: The word "alchemist" comes from the word "alchemy." It's etymology stems from the Greek word "khemeia," which means "the art of transmuting metals." It has been in use since ancient times. Alchemists can be considered the first chemists. They find ways to change metal to gold.

AML: A set of techniques, rules or regulations designed to disguise the process of earning money through unlawful or unacceptable conduct.

ANZ: The Australia and New Zealand Banking Group.

ArdVision: A secure hosted network used for board cooperation and the centralization of secure board records.

ASIC: The application-specific integrated circuit is an integrated circuit (IC) produced for a special purpose instead of being used for general purposes or applications.

ASX: Australian Securities Exchange.

Auroracoin: A cryptocurrency specifically created for the citizens of Iceland.

BITCOIN: A worldwide digital currency and digital payment network created and launched by an anonymous computer geek or set of geeks under the nickname Satoshi Nakamoto. It was launched as an open source program in 2009.

BITSTAMP: One the platforms that allows bitcoin exchanges. It is based in Luxembourg. Bitstamp creates room for trades between US dollars and bitcoins. It also allows for US dollar, Euro, Bitcoin, Ripple and Litecoin withdrawals and deposits.

BLOCKCHAIN: Traditionally, a continuously growing list of

ledgers referred to as blocks. These blocks are linked and secured through cryptography. A blockchain can be said to be a public ledger for every transaction carried out on Bitcoin's network.

BLOCKGEEKS: A community for blockchains in which one gains access to world-class talent, news and jobs.

BOARDROOM APPLICATION: This ensures capital, equity, entity and board of directors management solutions for both public and private organizations. Equity Enterprise could be dispersed through either a local means or a securely hosted system.

ANNALS: The historical activities of a country, organization or product.

BOOTSTRAPPING: A situation in which an entrepreneur begins an organization with little capital and then depends on monies other than external investments. An individual can be considered bootstrapping if they attempt to establish and build an organization from their personal money and savings or from the acquired revenues of the new organization. Bootstrapping also depicts a process used to calculate the zero-coupon yield curves received from market figures.

BOUGHT TECH: Blough Tech's main focus is computer systems, IT outsourcing converged communications and telephones.

BROKER: A person or business that requests a fee or commission after carrying out buying and selling orders initiated by an investor.

BURSTCOIN: A digital cryptographic currency and payment network built on blockchain technology.

BYTECODE: Also referred to as a portable code or p-code, this is a type of guideline or order set created for comprehensive implementation through a software translator. Unlike source codes readable by humans, bytecodes are numeric codes that are bounded. They are factors that are usually numeric addresses encoding the outcomes of compiler parsing and the semantic analysis of things such as the nesting depths of program objects, type and scope.

CASASCIUS COINS: Physical metal coins created by Bitcoin user Casascius. They were sold until November 26, 2013. They contained an embedded piece of paper with a digital Bitcoin value covered by a tamper-resistant hologram.

CEX STORES: An alternative hand goods chain in the United Kingdom. It specializes in video games, technology and computing. The store was created in London in 1992, and has grown since then. CEX has about 350 stores in the United Kingdom.

CHARGEBACK: A process in which funds are sent back to a consumer. It is used mainly in the United States and sometimes is forcibly carried out by the issuing bank of the instrument the consumer used to pay off an incurred debt. More importantly, it is the return of a prior outbound transfer of money from a user's bank account, line of credit or credit card.

CODIUS: A network for the secure execution of smart contracts and other smart features.

COINJAR: An advanced personal finance account that allows users to purchase, sell and transact with Bitcoin.

COMMONWEALTH BANK: An Australian multinational bank that does business all over New Zealand, Asia, the United Kingdom, Fiji and the United States.

CONSENSUS: A situation in which a middle ground in decision making is taken (that is, between total acceptance and a total discard).

CPU: The central processing unit is a computer component charged with responsibility and accountability in the translation, execution and implementation of many of the prompts from the system's other hardware and software.

CRYPTOCURRENCY: A virtual currency which uses cryptography for basic security measures. Because of this security structure, a counterfeit cryptocurrency is very hard to make.

CRYPTOGRAPH: A device used for encoding or decoding messages.

CRYPTONIGHT: A proof-of-work scheme created to accommodate ordinary system CPUs. However, at the moment, no specific purpose devices for mining are active. This means that CryptoNight can only be CPU-mined for the main time.

CURTAIL: To reduce or limit a thing, or prevent something from being completely exhausted.

DAO TOKEN: Created to operate as a platform that distributes funds in Ether, within the Ethereum network, to projects.

DATA61: Australia's leading digital research network

DIGISGIELD: Re-targets the difficulty of a coin to protect it from multi-pools and the excessive inflation of newly mined coins. DigiShield tries to re-target the difficulty of a coin within each block. In the case of Dogecoin and DigiByte, this happens every 60 seconds.

DIGITAL ASSET: A digitally kept commodity or online account

that an individual privately owns. Digital assets can be individual files like photos, videos, images and text format files.

DIGITAL CASH: A process of buying cash credits in somewhat small amounts as well as storing the credits in one's system. Digital cash can be spent in the process of conducting electronic transactions on the net. Theoretically, digital cash can be spent in very small increments, such as tenths of a cent or even less.

DOGECOIN: A digital currency that features a likeness of the Shiba Inu dog from Doge.

DOMAIN NAME: An identification program which serves as a category of sovereignty at the administrative level in relation to authority or control of power on the net. The names successfully registered in the DNS are referred to as domain names.

DOUBLESPENDING: Misappropriation within a digital cash network whereby the same single digital coin is spent more than once. This is possible because digital tokens contain some digital files which can be replicated or altered.

EMERCOIN: The mixture or cross infusion of Peercoin and Namecoin. Its blockchain provides room for a name-value storage network which includes an integrated server for .coin, .emc, .lib and .bazar domains.

ENOME.IO: E-Nome refers to an Australian private organization that has created a patent-pending program built using blockchain technology. The program enables consumers to be in charge of their personal medical files on their smartphones, integrating privacy and security.

ESCROW: A financial transaction program in which a third party is brought in to hold and monitor the payment of money between two parties in a transaction.

ETHER: An important element of and propellant for the smooth operation of the widely distributed application network Ethereum. It is also a medium of payment a customer makes within the platform to the machines processing the required operations.

ETHEREUM: An open-source and public blockchain based on a distributed computing network that features smart contracts.

FIAT CURRENCY: Legal tender with a value reinforced by a government responsible for its usage. For instance, the US dollar qualifies as a fiat currency. Other nationally and internationally recognized traditional currencies can also be classified as fiat currencies.

FTC (Federal Trade Commission): An autonomous organization of the United States government. It was established in 1914 through the Federal Trade Commission Act.

GPU: A graphics processing unit is a special electronic circuit designed to smoothly access and change a memory to speed up the generation of images in a frame buffer originally intended for output into a display machine.

GRIDCOIN: An open source network protocols which uses blockchain technology.

GUI: A graphical user interface (pronounced "gooey") is a user interface consisting of graphical elements like icons, buttons and windows.

HARDFORK: In relation to blockchain technology, a hard fork is a rapid turnaround to a protocol which helps regularize previously faulty blocks/transactions, and vice-versa. This also means that users' nodes must be upgraded to the latest version of the software's network.

HASH: An algorithm is capable of turning a considerably large amount of data into a hash with a fixed length. This particular hash is bound to keep emerging from the same data, though changing the data by a single margin would change the hash completely. Just like other computer-based data, hashes are quite large in number and are usually written in hexadecimals.

IBM: International Business Machines.

INTELLECTUAL PROPERTY: The creation of one's mind, such as literary and creative skills, names and ideas used in commerce, conceptions, symbols and discoveries.

IOT: The Internet of Things can be described as a system of correlative computing difficulties, creatures, articles, manuals and digital machines or populaces provided with a single identifier as well as the ability to pass on data within a network without the involvement of human-to-computer or human-to-human interactions.

IPFS: A process designed to provide a decentralized and indefinite technique for keeping and designating files.

LIMPID: Calm and untroubled.

LITECOIN: A peer-to-peer digital currency and very accessible software program released under the MIT/X11 permit. The creation and circulation of coins built upon a cryptographic policy which cannot be held by a central administrator. It also ensures concise and almost no payment costs to anyone around the world.

METAPHYSICIAN: A philosopher, within an academic circle, whose field of research or specialization is metaphysics – that is, research into the basic dimension of reality as well as the existence of humans and nature. "Meta" signifies "beyond." Therefore, meta-physical means those things positioned beyond or surpassing the normal physical dimension.

MICROPAYMENT: A financial transaction, occurring primarily online, involving a very small amount of money.

MINERS: Geeks who carry out complicated calculations referred to as hashes.

MINING BLOCKS: Mining is a task involving the annexation of transaction records into Bitcoin's ledger of previous transactions. The record of previous transactions is known as the blockchain because it is a chain of multiple blocks. The blockchain is used to confirm transactions, as it provides notifications that a transaction has occurred.

MINING: The process by which transactions are confirmed and directed to a public ledger referred to as a blockchain. It is also the process through which recent bitcoins are produced. Any curious individual with a good connection to the net and standard or basic hardware can participate in the mining process.

NETKI: A provider of unimpeded wellspring and easily accessible standard solutions for a blockchain.

NODES: An elementary component used in computer science. Nodes are data junctions on a wide network. Gadgets like cell phones, personal computers and printer are all different types of nodes. Generally, nodes are things that possess IP addresses.

NOTARY: A form of openly commissioned authority. It is also referred to as a "notary public." The main function of a notary is to operate as an impartial verifier during the signing of legal files. Notaries cannot reject witnesses to a transaction or document based on citizenship, race, gender or religion.

NVIDIA: Nvidia Corporation is a technological organization based in Santa Clara, California. It is responsible for designating processing units and graphics for gaming and professional marts.

OPENCOIN: OpenCoin's innovation originates from Ripple. It is a payment network which allows users to exchange any currency around the world. It has been cited as the very first open payment platform.

PAPER WALLETS: A form of document comprising all the information necessary to create an endless number of Bitcoin's private keys.

PAYOUTS: The measure of time in which an investment or project is anticipated to recover its incipient capital investment and become least profitable.

PEERCOIN: Also called PPCoin or PPC; it is a P2P cryptocurrency that uses both stake and work structures.

PIVOTAL: Of crucial importance.

PIXIE DUST: An enchanting golden glitter-like powder that confers the power of flight.

POLONIEX: A pure crypto-to-crypto transaction platform based in the United States. It was redesigned in early 2015 and has annexed an abundance of features to provide an entirely immersive trading experience.

POLYCOIN: A crypto payment administrative network for online businesses.

PREMINE: A premine or instamine is a situation in which the

developer or developers do not discharge the crypto currency in what can be regarded as an honest procedure.

PRIVATE KEY: A refined form of cryptography that permits a user to access their cryptocurrency. A private key is an inherent aspect of Bitcoin and altcoins, and its security composition helps safeguard a consumer from theft and unauthorized accessibility of the user's coins.

PUBLIC KEY: A cryptographic set of codes which permits a user to accept digital currencies into their account(s). The public key and private key are crucial tools for ensuring the security of the cryptocurrency economy.

PUTINCOIN: A decentralized cryptocurrency similar to Bitcoin.

QUANTUM COMPUTER: A computer which employs the quantum states of subatomic elements to accumulate and keep pieces of information.

RICHTOPIA: A finished media brand encompassing effective leadership, emerging technologies and global economies.

RIPPLE CRYPTOCURRENCY: A technology that performs as both a cryptocurrency and a digital payment platform for financial businesses.

SCALING/SCALABILITY: Scalability can be described as a feature of a system, model or function which describes its capability to cope with and perform under an intensified or expanding workload. A system that scales appropriately is able to regulate and increase its performance level or efficiency when put to test by larger operational requests.

SCRIBBLE: To write – for example, a note – hurriedly and without attention to its style or legibility.

SCRYPT ALGORITHM: A password-based key creation scheme developed by Colin Percival for the Tarsnap online backup service. The program was created to make large-scale custom hardware attacks expensive to carry out due to the need for large amounts of memory space.

SEC: The Securities and Exchange Commission is a federal agency of the United States government responsible for protecting investors as well as maintaining fair and orderly functions of security markets. The SEC also helps facilitate capital formations.

SEGREGATED WITNESS: SegWit is a procedure in which the limit of block size on a blockchain is raised by erasing signature data from the transactions. As soon as some sections of a transaction are erased, more space is available to enlist additional transactions to the chain.

SHA 256: Secure Hash Algorithm is a unit of cryptographic hash functions created and developed by the United States National Security Agency.

Slock.it: A company that integrates blockchain with the Internet of Things (IoT), thereby creating a decentralized and secure way for renters and owners to pay for and have access to anything that has been rented.

SSL: Secure Sockets Layer is a typical security measure for creating encrypted links between a server and a browser when operating on the web.

STM: A branch of Consortium E-Learning Network Pvt. Ltd. (CELNET). It produces hundreds of multidisciplinary examined journals in the fields of science, medicine and technology.

TANGENT: A line that meets a circle at a particular point. It is usually perpendicular to a radius dragged to the point of tangency.

TANGLE: An innovative blockless distributed record that is lightweight and scalable and that, for the first time ever, allows for the exchange of values without a fee.

TIM: Tradle's SDK which creates room for real-time messaging as well as an option for those messages to be permanently embedded in the blockchain. The messages could be straightforward or reconstructed. TiM is optimized to work effectively on smartphones, servers and desktops.

TIMESTAMP: A series of characters or encoded information which recognizes the time a certain action or event happened. It provides the accurate or almost accurate date and time of transactions.

UNDERWRITERS: Part of the initial public offering (IPO) process within the equity market. They are also a faction of the insurance application process. Underwriters are individual units responsible for examining and adopting other individual units' risks for fees like interest, spread, commission or even premium.

VIRTUAL: A thing that does not exist in the physical sense but that has been developed to appear to physically exist.

VOLATILITY: A statistical metric describing the dissemination of returns for a specific security. Usually, higher volatility increases security risks.

YEN: The authorized currency of Japan. It is the third most traded currency in the world.

REFERENCES

Protocol documentation

https: //en .Bitcoin .it /wiki /Protocol documentation

Bitcoin interviews

https: //www .cryptocoinsnews .com /bitcoin - interviews/

Vinny Lingham – Blockchain ID will make world a better place to live

https: //www .cryptocoinsnews .com /blockchain –id –will –make –world –better –place –live –vinny -lingham/

Useful notes Bitcoin

http: //tvtropes .org /pmwiki /pmwiki .php /UsefulNotes /Bitcoin

Protocol documentation

https: //enbitcoin .it /wiki /Protocol documentation

Mastering Bitcoin

http: //chimera .lab oreilly .com /books /1234000001802 /ch07 .html# introduction 2

An interview with Satoshi Nakamoto

https: //medium .com /@Ulrich 98986 /an –interview –with –satoshi –nakamoto –the –inventor –of –blockchain -c638dff03c2e

Two early Bitcoin developers who worked directly with Satoshi Nakamoto

https: //qz .com /675830 /two –early –bitcoin –developers – who –worked –directly –with –satoshi –nakamoto –weigh –in –on –his –real - identity/

Notes on Bitcoin

https: //www .oskarth .com /notes –on - bitcoin/

The extended Bitcoin network

http: //chimera .labs .oreilly .com /books /1234000001802 /ch06 .html# the extended bitcoin network

A Bitcoin analysis and the hunt for Satoshi

http: //www .firstpost .com /tech /news –analysis /a –bitcoin – chronology –and –the –hunt –for –satoshi-nakamoto –over – the –years -3681113 .html

Bitcoin growth fund – Invest in high growth startups

https: // bitcoingrowthfund .com/

How many people own Bitcoin or Ethereum

https: //hankyulpark .wordpress .com /2017/03 /24 /how – many –people –in –the –world –own –bitcoin –or - ethereum/

Bitcoin millionaires

https: //bitconnect .co /bitcoin –news /254 /bitcoin – millionaires –how –many –people –hold –all –the –worlds - bitcoins/

https://bitconnect.co/cdn-

cgi/l/chk_jschl?jschl_vc=83bcb78fa4eb556fc1081e335fd6b732
&pass=1502796786.539-fWHydSU1kB&jschl_answer=1232139

What estimate of individuals own Bitcoin

https: //bitcoin .stackexchange .com /questions /50849
/beginning -2017 —what —estimate —of —individuals —own -
bitcoin

How many people use Bitcoin

https: //www .quora .com /How —many —people —use -bitcoin

What is Ethereum

https:// blockgeeks .com/guides /what – is - ethereum/

Trading Zcash

https: //www .coindesk .com /investors —know —trading –
zcash /

How zk-snarks work in Zcash

https: // z .cash /technology /zksnarks .html

Zcash developers- Zcash community

https: //www .zcash community .com / developers/

Getting started with Zcash

https: //z .cash /blog /getting —started —developing .html

AURBTC chart and quotes cryptocurrency Auroracoin

https: // www .tradingview .com /symbols / AURBTC/

Introduction to proof of stake

http: //old .peercointalk .org /index .php ? topic = 3674.0

Peercoin-secure and sustainable cryptocoin

https: // peercoin . net/

Whitepaper- Peercoin

https: //peercoin .net /whitepaper

What is Peercoin? Intro and important links

https: //talk .peercoin .net/t /what – is –peercoin –intro – important –links /2889 /8

Scrypt mining – Bitcoin | altcoin

http: //bitcoin –vs .s3 .amazonaws .com /bitcoin –altcoin – scrypt –mining –rig .html

Litecoin equally good or better than Bitcoin

https: //seekingalpha .com /amp /article /4086771 – litecoin – equally –good –better -bitcoin

Bitcoin overwview

https: //www .cryptocompare .com /coins/doge /overview /BTC

Burstcoin forum

http://forums. Burst –team .us/

Dash (cryptocurrency) – Wikipedia

https:// en .m. Wikipedia .org /wiki /Dash _ (cryptocurrency)

Notes l breaking Bitcoin

http:// www. Breaking bitcoin .com / category /notes/

Dash crypto intro for techies

https:// www. slideshare.net/ mobile /JosephHolbrook Vetera /dash- crypto- currency-I ntro- f

IOTA – Next generation blockchain

https://iota.org/

https://iota.org/ techies

IOTA support – The IOTA foundation

https://iotasupport .com / foundation. Shtml

IOTA foundation – Beyond blockchain meetup Chicago

https: // www. Meetup .com/ Chicago- IOTA- Meetup/

ZK-SNARKS technically said: basic principles – coinfabrik

https:// blog .coinfabrik .com/ zk- snarks- said- basic-principles/

Introduction to ZK-SNARKS with examples – consensys

https:// media. Consensys .net /introduction –to –zk snarks – with – examples -3283b554fc3b? gi=63bbe22a2ee8

Dash the first decentralized autonomous organization

https:// cointelegraph.com/news/ dash-the- first-decentralized- autonomous- organization

Zcash 6 month anniversary special milestones

https:// cointelegraph. Com /news /zcash -6 – month – anniversary –special –milestones -100 -mln- market –cap – vision

How ZK-SNARKS work in Zcash

https://z.cash/ technology /zksnarks.html

https:// z.cash/ team. Html

All blog posts

https://z. cash/ blog/

https:// z.cash/ blog/ helloworld. Html

Zksnarks and blockchain scalability

https:// hackernoon .com/ zksnarks –and –blockchain - scalability- af85e350a93a? gi= 185dbded0d7c

Could Monero implement zksnarks in the future?

https:// monero. Stackexchange .com/ questions/ 2523/ could- monero –implement -zk- snarks- in- the –future

Why are zk-snarks possible in laymans terms

https://crypto .stackexchange .com/ questions /37581 /why- are -zk-snarks –possible –in –laymans –terms /37582

How xrp compares to Bitcoin and Ethereum

https:// ripple .com/ insights /xrp- compares –btc -eth/

Bitcoin rival Ripple is sitting on many billions of dollars

https:// www. cnbc .com /2017 /05 /26 /bitcoin –rival –ripple –is –sitting –on –many –billions –of – dollars – of –xrp .html

Aurora wiki l Wikipedia Auroracoin 2017

http:// fireworks 2017. com/ news /auroracoin –wiki

Finance and news trends

http: // auroracoin. org/

Auroracoin AUR: Coin of view

http:// coinofview .com/ coin/ Auroracoin .html

Auroracoin AUR information

https: // cryptocurrencytalk .com/ topic/ 4223 -auroracoin- aur –information /? Page =2

1.0 user guide Zcash wiki/wiki

https: // github . com / zcash/ zcash / wiki/ 1.0- User -Guide

Github / Aurarad/ Auroracoin current Auroracoin source

https: // github .com /aurarad /Auroracoin

Peercointalk.org

http: // old .peercointalk .org / index .php ? topic =3674.0

GHVD Goed. Hart Voor Dieren

http: // goedhartvoordieren .nl/ ? page =r%2Fpeercoin%2F

Weercoin resources

http: // peerco .in /resources .php

What is Peercoin cryptocurrency ?

http: //heavy .com /tech /2013 /12 /what –is –peercoin - cryptocurrency/

Peercoin quora the new world order

http: // www .altcoin –mining .com/ peercoin –quora- the- new- world –order –maybe - yocoin/

https:// www. coinpursuit .com/ crypto –currency / peercoin- ppc .33/

Blockchain | Peercoin assets

https: //tokenmarket .net/ blockchain/ peercoin/ assets/ peercoin/

https ://www .digitalgain .net / blog/ peercoin/

The controversial child of Peercoin and Litecoin

https: // 99bitcoins .com / novacoin –the –controversial –child –of –peercoin –and –litecoin -infographic/

Introduction to Peercoin

http :// cointhttps: //talk. Peercoin .net /t/ introduction –to – peercoin /3159rader .org/ peercoin –proof –of –stake –and - bitcoin/

The complete guide to minting

https: // talk .peercoin .net /t/ the – complete –guide - to-minting/ 2524

http: // www .coins2day .com/ peercoin –howto .html

http: // poscalculator .peercointalk .org/

Peercoin minting facts

http: // wiki. peercointalk. Org /index .php ? title = Peercoin _minting _facts

Getting started – Peercoin

https: // www2 .coinmine .pl /ppc / index .php ? page = gettingstarted

Newcomers – Peercoin

https: // peercoin .net / newcomers

https: // peercoin .net /minting

Ripple – Big bank

https: // www .coindesk .com/ ripple – big -bank- blockchains/

10 things you need to know about Ripple

https: // www .coindesk .com /10-things – you –need –to – know –about -ripple/

Price of Iceland's Auroracoin falls 50% against Bitcoin

https: // www .coindesk .com / price –iceland –auroracoin – fall - 50- bitcoin -airdrop/

Cryptocurrency Auroracoin given to person in Iceland

https: //www .coindesk .com/ cryptocurrency –auroracoin –

every –person –iceland /

How Peercoin got a boost from Bitcoins halving

https: // www .coindesk .com/ how- peercoin- got -a- boost –
from -bitcoins- halving/

Emercoin group announces set of blockchain features

https: // www. coindesk .com /press –releases /emercoin –
blockchain –banking -sector/

About Emercoin

https: //support .xbtce .info /Knowledgebase / Article / View
/159/78/ about – emercoin

Emercoin coin – distributed blockchain services for businesses

http: // https :// emercoin .com/ getstarted

All you need to know about Emercoin

ftreporter .com / all -you- need –to –know –about -emercoin/

Emercoin (EMC) price, charts market cap and others

https: // coinmarketcap .com /currencies / emercoin/

Is Emercoin the future of blockchain technology?

https: // ghost .report /2017/ 05/31 /is – emercoin –the –
future –of –blockchain -technology/

Emercoin review – EMC personal and business distributed blockchain

https: //bitcoinexchangeguide .com /emercoin/

IOTA – Promise of a bright crypto future

https: //medium .com/ @cryptojudgement/ iota –promise –of
–a – bright –crypto –future -6b7517349e32

A note on Zcash

https : // medium .com/ @jimmysong/ a- note –on –zcash -
7514d6be6312

Zk-snarks – Under the hood

https:// medium .com / @VitalikButerin/ zk-snarks- under -
the- hood- b33151a013f6

Zero knowledge – The future of privacy

https:// medium .com /blockchannel /episode -3 – zero –
knowledge -the- future –of -privacy- ea18479295f4

In Satoshi's footsteps – The Emercoin developers have announced complete decentraliztion

https: // medium .com /@emer .tech/ in- satoshis- footsteps –
the –emercoin –developers –have –announced - the- complete
– decentralization –of -82ba18376d97

Emercoin – Setting the new standard for top blockchains

https: // news .bitcoin .com/ emercoin –setting –the – new –
standard –for –top -blockchains/

Is Zcash mining profitable?

https: //www .quora .com/ Is –Zcash –mining –profitable

Should I start mining Bitcoin or should I continue mining Zcash?

https: // www .quora. com / Should- I- start – mining – Bitcoin –or – should –I – continue –mining – Zcash

What is Zcash

https: //www .quora .com/ What – is –zcash

What's good and bad about Zcash

https: //www. quora .com /Whats –good –and -bad- about – zcash

Is Zcash another altcoin

https: //www .quora .com /Is –zcash –another –altcoin

What could be the future value of Ripple XRP

https: //www .quora .com /What –could –be –the –future – value –of –Ripple –XRP – Cryptocurrency

Is Ripple better than Ethereum

https: //www .quora .com/ Is – Ripple –better - than- Ethereum – What – are – the – technical – and – fundamental – differences

Is Ripple XRP the next bandwagon to jump onto

https: //www .quora .com / Is – Ripple – XRP – the –next – bandwagon – to – jump – onto – for – those –who –missed – the –Bitcoin –flight –What –do –you –anticipate –the –future –of – Ripple – Labs –to –be ? redirected_ qid= 15184222

How is Ripple different from Bitcoin

https:// www .quora .com / How –is –Ripple –different - from-bitcoin

What is the feature value of Ripple coins

https://· www .quora .com /What –is –the –feature –value –of –Ripple –coins

What is Auroracoin

https: //www .quora .com /What –is – Auroracoin

Digital currency – How do I mine Auroracoin

https: // www .quora .com /Digital – Currency –How –do –I -mine- auroracoin

How can you trade an Auroracoin

https: // www .quora .com /How – can –you –trade – an –Auroracoin

Peercoin

https: // www .quora .com /topic / Peercoin

Where can I buy and sell Peercoin

https: // www .quora .com / Where – can - I- buy –and –sell – Peercoin

Emercoin – All questions

https: // www .quora .com /topic / Emercoin /all_ questions

What are the unique features of Emercoin

https: // www .quora . com/ unanswered /What – are –the – unique –features –of –Emercoin

What is Burstcoin

https: // www .quora .com / Whats – Burstcoin

Do you recommend me to invest in Burstcoin

https: // www .quora .com/ Do –you – recommend - me- to – invest –in – Burstcoin

Which is better Siacoin or Burstcoin

https: // www .quora .com / Which – is –better –siacoin – or – burstcoin

https: // www. quora .com / topic / Burstcoin

How scalable is Iota

https: //www. reddit .com /r/ Iota/ comments /6h3lyn/ how_ scalable _is _iota/

What does zec aim to achieve – whats its long term

https: //www .reddit .com /r/ zec /comments /6dsp1z /what _does _zec _aim _to _ achieve _whats _its _long _term/

What advantages does Ripple have over Bitcoin

https: // www .reddit .com /r/ Ripple /comments /2qdxko /what _advantages _does _ripple _have _over _bitcoin/

https: // www .reddit .com /r/ auroracoin/

How much can I earn from 1tb hdd

https: // www .reddit .com /r/ burstcoin / comments /6tcy99 /how _much _can _i _ earn _from _1tb _hdd _that _i _ salvage/

Burstcoin

https: // www .reddt .com /r/ burstcoin/

Pop up: Burst faucet: All the burstcoin faucets

http: // www .burstfaucet .ml /2017 /03 /welcome –to – burstfaucet .html ?m =1

How to mine zcash ZEC

https: //www. cryptocompare .com /mining /guides /how –to – mine –zcash /

Burstcoin (BURST) BTC – overview, forum, live streaming

https: // www .cryptocompare .com / coins / burst /post /p_ 4923/

Burstcoin (BURST) – How to mine Burst (HDD mining)

https: //www .cryptocompare .com / coins/ burst /post /p_ 4923/ BTC

The official Burstcoin cryptocurrency hub

https: // www .burstnation .com/

Crowdfunding and projects

https: //www .burstnation .com /wbb /index .php ? board /14 – crowdfunding –and –projects /

Burst features

https: // www .burstnation .com /wbb / index . php? Board /11

–burst –features /

An amateur's notes on cryptocurrency

https: // steemit .com / cryptocurrency /@cheah /an –amateur –s –notes –on –cryptocurrency

Burst – What is it

https: // steemit .com / cryptocurrency / @lexicon / burst – what –is – it

Which will be the dominating scalable coin? (NEM vs IOTA)

https: // bitcointalk .org / index .php ? topic =1965832.20

Auroracoin – Empowering financial freedom

https: // bitcointalk .org / index . php ? topic =1044432.0

Auroracoin – A cryptocurrency for iceland

https: // bitcointalk .org / index .php ? topic = 1467050.0

https: // bitcointalk .org / index .php ? topic = 446062.0

Is anyone turning profit with Burst mining

https: // bitcointalk .org / index .php ? topic = 1756227.0

Burstcoin [BUSRT] price speculation

https: // bitcointalk .org / index .php ? topic =1513328.20

AURBTC – Chat and quotes cryptocurrencies Auroracoin

https:// www .tradingview .com /symbols /AURBTC /

Burstcoin – Chat and quotes online | Trading view

Burstcoin hub

http:// burst .msft .online/

CIYAM – AT documentation index

http: // ciyam .org /at/

CIYAM – AT use case: Atomic cross chain transfer

Bursctcoin Wikipedia

https:// en .m. Wikipedia .org / wiki / Burstcoin

Interview with Burst team, Burst general discussion

https:// www. burstnation .com /wbb /index .php ? thread /1553 –interview –with –burst –team / &page No =1

Rig setup questions – mining and plotting – the official burstnation website

https: //www .burstnation .com/ wbb /index .php ? thread /2198 –rig –setup –questions / & page No =1

Gavs guides [crypto: burstcoin]

https: // wiki .gavowen .ninja /doku .php ? id = crypto:burstcoin

Burstcoin – currency: Burst: Real time price indices

https: // bravenewcoin .com /burstcoin#Trading –Pairs

Crytocoin .cc: Burstcoin (burst)

http: // cryptocoin .cc/table. Php ? cryptocoin= burstcoin

The crowdfunding center – Big data driven crowdfunding

http: // mobile .thecrowdfundingcenter .com /projects .php ?
id = 0168X2

DogeChain online dogecoin wallet

https: // my .dogechain .info /#/ loading

Features from the most popular altcoins

https: // bitcoinmagazine .com /articles /features –from –the –
most –popular –altcoins –are –planned –for –bitcoin -
1463675591/

Dogecoin news and features, WIRED UK

http://www.wired.co.uk/topic/dogecoin

Dogechain – The official Dogechain explorer

https: // dogechain .info/

An interview with the inventor of Dogecoin

http: //junkee .com/ an –interview –with –the –inventor –of –
dogecoin –the –internets –favourite –new –currency /27411

Dogecoin creators talk surprising success

http: //www .ibtimes .co.uk /dogecoin –creators –talk –
surprising –success –scams –future –pronunciation -1435604

The humans behind dogecoin – spelhunk.in

http: // spelunk .in /2013 /12 /17 /discover –dogecoin –
currency –for –the -internet/

The co-creator of Dogecoin talks...

https: // techcrunch .com /2014 /06 /27 / the –co –creator –of –dogecoin –talks –about –building – one –of –the –funniest – and –most –popular –cryptocurrencies –in – the- world /

Dogecoins and its IBM developer...

http: // www .dailytech .com /Dogecoins +and + Its + IBM + Developer + Ride + Meme + to + 130M + Fortune /article33960 .html

List of major fundraising events – Burstcoin archives...

http: // dogecoin .wikia .com/ wiki / List_ of _Major _Fundraising _Events

Burstcoin archives Crytocoin news

Burstcoin

https: // www .cryptocoinsnews .com /tag /burstcoin/

Five reasons why the Dogecoin price should rebound soon

https: //www .cryptocoinsnews .com /five –reasons -why- the- dogecoin –price –should –rebound -soon/

Dogecoin transactions per day exceed cap

https: // www .cryptocoinsnews .com / dogecoin –transactions –exceed –market -cap/

The advantages and features of Gridcoin

http: // wiki .gridcoin .us /Advantages _% 26 _Featurez

Gridcoin value for research l Gridcoin chaser

http: // bitcoinchaser .com /gridcoin –review

DogeChain wallet issue #27 Dogecoin/dogecoin.com

https: // github .com /dogecoin /dogecoin .com /issues /27

https: // github .com/ gridcoin /Gridcoin –Research /blob /master /README .md

Gridcoin (GRC) first coin utilizing BOINC – official thread

https: // bitcointalk .org/ index .php ? topic =324118.0

Is Gridcoin the future of Altcoins?

https: // bitcointalk .org/ index .php ? topic =371496.0

Gridcoin: The cryptocurrency of the future

http: // www .thecryptocurrent .com/ ? p =76

Gridcoin news – cointelegraph

https: // cointelegraph .com/ tags/ gridcoin

Gridcoin – cryptocurrency of scientific distributed computing

https: // themerkle .com/ gridcoin –cryptocurrency –scientific –distributed -computing/

DigiByte with Jared Tate

https: //m .mixcloud .com /CryptoAfterDark /episode -2 – digibyte –with –jared –tate - s2e02/

Lifeboat foundation bios. Jared Tate

https: // lifeboat .com /ex /bios .jared .tate

Dogecoin (doge) – BTC dogecoin (DOGE) – live stream

https: // www. cryptocompare .com /coins /doge /overview /BTC

DogeChain web wallet – review and features

https: //www .cryptocompare .com /wallets /dogechain /

DigiByte (DGB) RevEx review favourite cryptocurrency

Digibot: Telegram | digibyte global blockchain

https:// www .blackhatworld .com /seo /thoughts –on – digibyte .939324/

Cliff notes please – Burstcoin

https: //www .reddit .com /r /burstcoin /comments /6j5m1b /cliff _notes _please/

Podcast interview with Billy Markus

https: //www .reddit .com/r /dogecoin /comments /1wnj7b /podcast _interview _with _billy _markus _find _out _ what/

How long does dogechain transactions take to confirm?

https: //www .reddit .com/r /dogecoin /comments /5jj5f1 /how _long _does _dogecoin _transactions _to _ confirm/

Should I invest in Gridcoin

https: // www .reddit .com /r/ gridcoin /comments /2m048w /should _i _invest _in _ gridcoin/

What is Gridcoin and how to get started

https: // www .reddit .com/r /gridcoin /comments /48bes0 /what _is _ gridcoin _and _how _to _get _ started/

About the future of Gridcoins

https: //www .reddit .com /r /gridcoin /comments /401f8s /how _do _you _feel _about _the _future _of _ gridcoins/

How Digibyte is different

https: // www .reddit .com /r /DigiByte /comments /6fo9wi /can _someone _explain _how _digibyte _is _different/

DigiByte daily discussion thread

https: //www .reddit .com /r /DigiByte /comments /6kz9zi /digibyte _daily _discussion _ thread _070317/

GRC BTC – Chart and quotes cryptocurrencies – Gridcoin

https://www .tradingview .com /symbols / GRCBTC/

http:// ftreporter .com /digibyte –a –decentralized –blockchain -platform/

The blockchain technology

http: // scet .berkeley .edu / blockchain -technology/

A maturity model for blockchain adoption l Spingerlink

https: //link .springer .com /article /10.1186 /s40854 -016-0031-z

Blockchain technology – A futuristic solution to conservations greatest challenges

http: //blog .conservation .org /2017 /08 /in –blockchain – technology –a –futuristic –solution –to –conservations – greatest - challenges/

Long live Dogecoin – why developers won't let the joke die

https: //www .coindesk .com/ dogecoin- is –the –joke –that – wouldn't –die –finally -dying/

Credit Suisse report explores blockchain impact

https:// www .coindesk .com /credit –suiss –blockchain – impact –stock - performance/

Gridcoin founder talks revolution mining

http: //www .guugll .eu /gridcoin –founder –talks –revolution - mining/

Author's Note

Thank you again for purchasing this book!

I hope this book was able to help you learn more about cryptocurrencies.

Finally, if you enjoyed this book, then I'd like to ask you for a favor, would you be kind enough to leave a review for this book on Amazon? It'd be greatly appreciated!

Good luck!

Made in the USA
San Bernardino, CA
04 December 2017